P.E.T.S.™

Primary Education
Thinking Skills - 2
Curriculum

Jody Nichols, Sally Thomson, Margaret Wolfe, Dodie Merritt
Illustrated by Dodie Merritt

Pieces of Learning

CLC0221
ISBN 978-1-880505-37-3
Cover Design by John Steele
© Illustrations by Dodie Merritt
© 1998 Pieces of Learning
www.piecesoflearning.com
Marion IL 62959

Printed by McNaughton & Gunn, Inc.
Saline MI
11/2009

Acknowledgments

The authors of this book would like to thank the administration of Illinois School Districts #47 and #424 for their support of the PETS program as well as the many primary teachers in whose classes these materials were field-tested.

We would like to thank Nancy Johnson for inspiring Max and Yolanda's Figural Nursery Rhymes and for the use of Jack and Jill and Little Miss Muffett.

Many thanks as well to our families for their continued patience and support.

TABLE OF CONTENTS

PETS™ (Primary Education Thinking Skills)

Dudley the Detective

Isabel the Inventor

Sybil the Scientist

Yolanda the Yarnspinner

Max the Magician

Jordan the Judge

DEFINITION

...is a systematized enrichment and diagnostic thinking skills program that can be easily integrated into an existing primary curriculum. P.E.T.S.™ serves the dual purpose of helping in the identification of academically talented learners and teaching students higher level thinking skills.

PROGRAM RATIONALE

P.E.T.S.™ follows the taxonomy outlined by Benjamin Bloom, presenting lessons in analysis, synthesis, and evaluation. These higher order skills are less emphasized in most primary curricula, yet students of all ability levels have shown interest in and understanding of these different types of thinking.

P.E.T.S.™ also provides teachers with the opportunity to identify talented learners early in their school careers and to implement a curriculum which will best suit their special needs. This identification occurs in the classroom setting.

The format of the P.E.T.S.™ delivery system follows a modification of the Triad Model posed by Dr. Joseph Renzulli. The entire class is given the opportunity to experience the challenge of the thinking skills. Based on teacher observation and student interest, a small group of students is then given further opportunity to explore the thinking skills in a variety of in-depth activities. During the small group activities, the teacher is able to evaluate student potential further and to plan student programming accordingly.

PROGRAM OVERVIEW

P.E.T.S.™ has a two-tier delivery system which is easily facilitated by the classroom teacher or a visiting specialist. The first tier focuses on whole class enrichment activities for the entire grade level population. The second tier activities are used in small group settings to challenge the more capable students.

PRIMARY EDUCATION THINKING SKILLS I introduces six characters, each with a special thinking strategy:

> Dudley the Detective — deductive logic
> Sybil the Scientist — analytical thinking
> Isabel the Inventor — inventive thinking
> Yolanda the Yarnspinner — creative thinking
> Max the Magician — visual perception
> Jordan the Judge — evaluative thinking

PRIMARY EDUCATION THINKING SKILLS I lays a strong foundation for **PRIMARY EDUCATION THINKING SKILLS 2** but is not a necessary prerequisite.

PRIMARY EDUCATION THINKING SKILLS 2 is a more complex development of the thinking strategies and introduces students to the terms convergent, divergent, visual, and evaluative thinking. Through stories and a series of whole class activities, the four units reintroduce the characters, each with its own special thinking strategy and goes on to show how the characters blend their thinking skills as they work together to solve problems. Additional activities are provided for small group lessons. These activities stimulate students with high-interest, challenging activities, many of which are hands-on. Detailed lesson plans are provided for all whole class and small group lessons.

Parallel to the instruction element of P.E.T.S.™ is a two-tier diagnostic tool for identifying talented learners. A behavioral checklist that is used by the classroom teacher during the whole group lessons provides information about students who show potential for each thinking strategy. Students demonstrating outstanding aptitude during the whole class lessons, as recorded on the checklist, are invited to participate in the small group lessons. A more detailed checklist is used during the small group lessons to better identify student levels of talent and abilities.

The **PETS 2**™ program is comprised of:

> — twelve lessons for the whole class
> — twelve activities for the small group
> — detailed lesson plans
> — diagnostic checklists

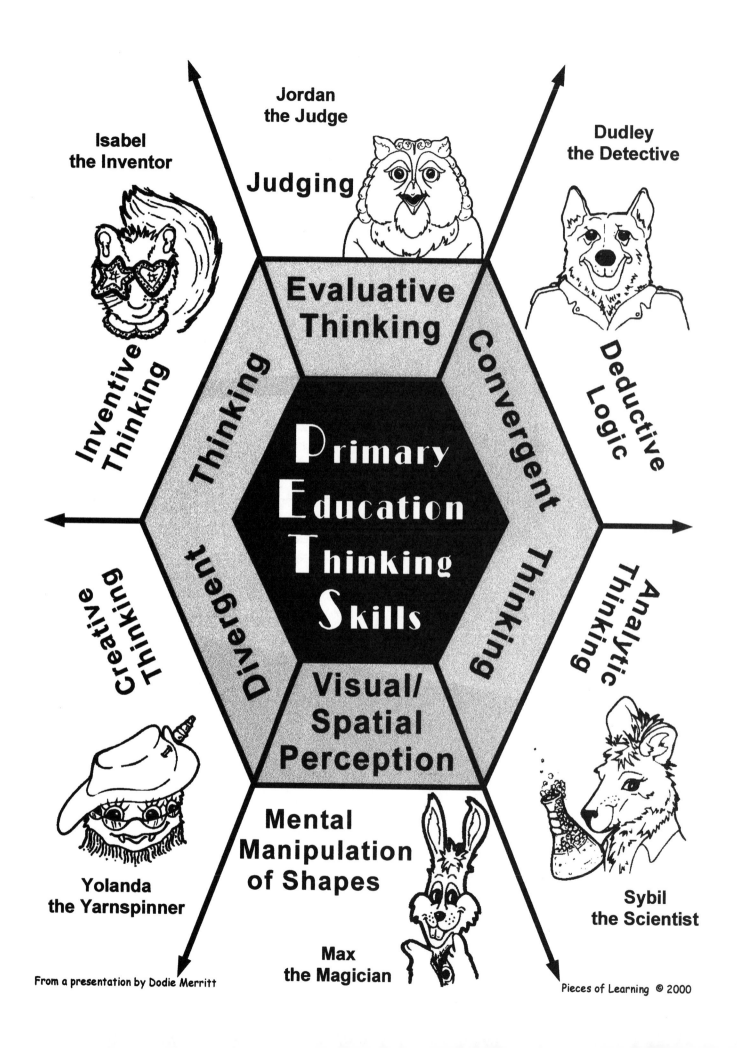

Isabel
the Inventor

Jordan
the Judge

Judging

Dudley
the Detective

Inventive Thinking

Thinking

Evaluative Thinking

Convergent Thinking

Deductive Logic

Primary Education Thinking Skills

Divergent

Creative Thinking

Visual/ Spatial Perception

Analytic Thinking

Yolanda
the Yarnspinner

Mental Manipulation of Shapes

Sybil
the Scientist

Max
the Magician

From a presentation by Dodie Merritt

IDENTIFYING TALENTED LEARNERS

The primary classroom teacher has a very diverse population in both maturity and intellect. Some students will immediately appear talented in certain areas and other students need to be given opportunities to show their abilities. Before attempting to use the checklists, teachers need to understand the different characteristics and behaviors which indicate that a student might be talented in a particular area.

CONVERGENT THINKING

One characteristic of students who excel at convergent thinking is the ability to arrive at the correct answer intuitively. They tend to see the interrelationships between clues and defer judgment until all clues have been collected. In addition, students who are able to analyze objects for various attributes as well as recognize flaws in reasoning demonstrate talent as convergent thinkers.

DIVERGENT THINKING

Those students who excel at divergent thinking are able to list many responses to questions or brainstorm many ideas. Not only are they fluent in their thinking but they may also exhibit flexibility. They tend to be original, giving off-beat and sometimes very humorous responses. These students can elaborate or expand upon an idea, adding intricate detail. An advanced vocabulary is sometimes displayed during the divergent thinking activities.

VISUAL THINKING

These students demonstrate a good memory for visual details. They may not be as verbal as their classmates and therefore may not have as much opportunity to demonstrate their talents during traditional classroom activities. These students often enjoy activities involving the mental manipulation of shapes and may respond well to visual images such as graphic organizers.

EVALUATIVE THINKING

The students who are able to evaluate and offer a solution that is based on valid considerations have an opportunity to shine during these specially designed lessons. The checklists support behaviors such as seeing more than one viewpoint, understanding criteria, and supporting decisions.

IDENTIFYING TALENTED LEARNERS DURING WHOLE CLASS LESSONS

The P.E.T.S.™ program can help both classroom and specialty teachers identify talented learners in whole class and small group settings. The whole class lessons are the first tier in identifying talented learners. The ideal situation is to have two teachers in the classroom, one teacher presenting the thinking skill lesson and one teacher observing students' behaviors. If two teachers are not available, a parent volunteer or a teacher's aide may assist the classroom teacher. If this is the case, the teacher can help the aide by using key phrases to indicate that a student's name should be added to the checklist. For example, a teacher may say, *"Wow, Julie, that's a great way to use an earlier clue to see the new clue."*

Six behavioral characteristics have been included for each thinking skill. These behaviors vary from thinking skill to thinking skill. *P.E.T.S.™ Behavioral Checklists* are provided in each unit as an easy reference for teachers. As a student is observed showing one of the behaviors, the teacher records the student's name in the appropriate box. If the student shows additional behaviors in the same category, the teacher can add check marks after the name. To differentiate between sessions, record each lesson's responses in a different color.

It is important for the teacher observing students to look beyond just the most vocal students who are the first to answer. All students need to be observed and questioned in order to give every student an opportunity to show his or her potential. There is a category on the *P.E.T.S.™ Behavioral Checklist* to indicate students who show outstanding performance on class work. The *P.E.T.S.™ Behavioral Checklists* also include an opportunity to list students who did not participate during the thinking skill lesson yet have shown the characteristics in other classroom situations.

It is essential for the teacher to remember that the number of talented learners in any one classroom may be quite small. The P.E.T.S.™ program has been designed to identify this small population; do not expect the entire class to achieve mastery of the lessons. **All students will benefit from exposure to these higher-level thinking skills; however, the actual number of students demonstrating mastery level may be quite small.** That's OK.

At the end of one, two, or three whole class thinking skill lessons, the students who are talented in that thinking strategy will stand out as the teacher examines the *P.E.T.S.™ Behavioral Checklist*. The students listed in a variety of areas and/or frequently on the *P.E.T.S.™ Behavioral Checklist* are invited to the small group lessons. The small group may vary from thinking skill to thinking skill.

IDENTIFYING TALENTED LEARNERS DURING SMALL GROUP LESSONS

The second tier of the identification process is the small group lesson. The small group may consist of students from a variety of classrooms or a group from the same classroom.

The small group lessons are designed to provide further enrichment and opportunities for teachers to observe additional behaviors that identify talented learners. The small group lessons are not as structured as the whole class lessons, providing students with more opportunities for interaction and cooperative problem solving. These lessons are intended to be diagnostic rather than instructional. The teacher assumes the role of observer and recorder as students work independently through the activities.

The *P.E.T.S.™ Small Group Checklist* on the following page is provided for record-keeping and note-taking during each small group lesson. Use one checklist for each group member. The student's checklist is cumulative, so the same checklist is used each time a student is a member of a small group.

It is helpful to fill out the student information on the *P.E.T.S.™ Small Group Checklist* before the group meets. The form is used to assess and identify talented learners. Any pertinent information or observations made during the small group lessons should be noted on the checklist. Not every characteristic is applicable to every lesson. Everything a student does can be viewed as diagnostic. At the end of the school year, the data from the *P.E.T.S.™ Small Group Checklist* will give teachers information to help identify talented learners.

PETS™ Small Group Checklist
A Cumulative Student Record

STUDENT: SCHOOL: TEACHER:

GRADE LEVEL:

CHARACTERISTICS	YEAR: DATE ACTIVITY + ✓ –	CONVERGENT			DIVERGENT			VISUAL			EVALUATIVE		
	Does difficult mental tasks												
	Retains information												
	Comprehends concepts												
	Sees interrelationships												
	Reasons independently												
	Makes evaluations												
	Reads above grade level												
	Uses an extensive vocabulary												
	Enjoys puzzles/problems with a twist												
	Uses alternative methods to solve problems												
	Displays an advanced sense of humor												
	Exhibits curiosity												
	Demonstrates leadership												
	Is fluent with ideas												
	Shows flexibility												
	Exhibits originality												
	Elaborates with many details												
	Demonstrates task commitment												

COMMENTS:

In this unit, students are presented with the concepts of convergent thinking. Dudley the Detective uses deductive thinking strategies to find the one right answer. Sybil the Scientist uses analytical thinking strategies to examine attributes and classify objects. Within a story setting, each character explains to the other how his or her thinking strategy works, and then the two convergent thinkers partner to share their skills on a third type of problem.

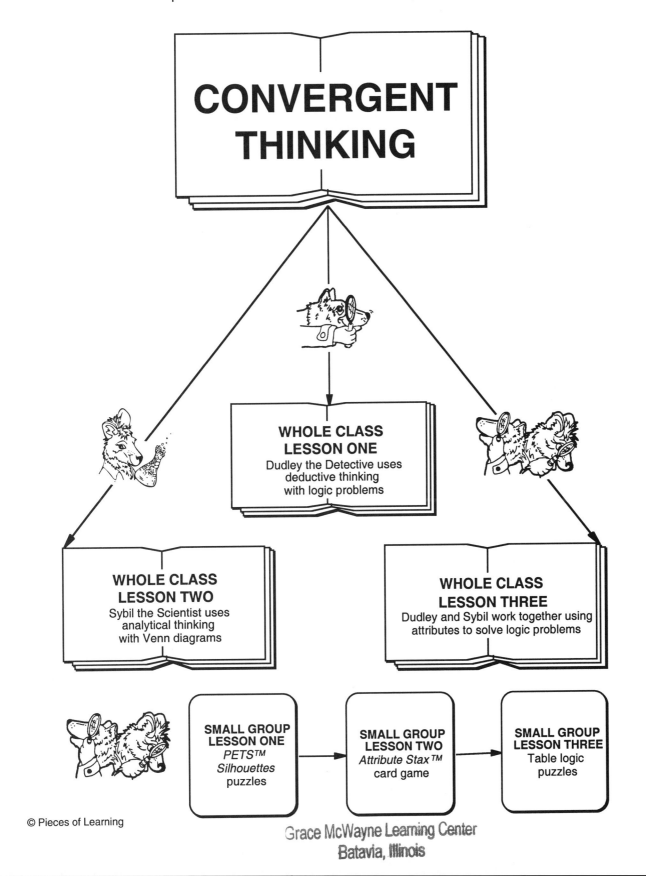

CONVERGENT THINKING

WHOLE CLASS LESSON ONE
Dudley the Detective uses deductive thinking with logic problems

WHOLE CLASS LESSON TWO
Sybil the Scientist uses analytical thinking with Venn diagrams

WHOLE CLASS LESSON THREE
Dudley and Sybil work together using attributes to solve logic problems

SMALL GROUP LESSON ONE
PETS™ Silhouettes puzzles

SMALL GROUP LESSON TWO
Attribute Stax™ card game

SMALL GROUP LESSON THREE
Table logic puzzles

Convergent Thinking

Grace McWayne Learning Center
Batavia, Illinois

PETS

Behavioral Checklist

Convergent Thinking
(Deductive Logic/Analysis)

List names of students as each behavior appears.

Add checkmarks after name if behavior is repeated.

Use a different color of ink or pencil for each whole group lesson.

Teacher _____
Grade: 1 ___ 2 ___ 3 ___

Date of whole   1. _____
group instruction 2. _____
                          3. _____

GRASPS CONCEPTS VERY QUICKLY	USES ONE CLUE TO DETERMINE ANOTHER OR PUTS CLUES TOGETHER -- **SEES INTERRELATIONSHIP OF CLUES**
RECOGNIZES FLAWED REASONING	GATHERS AND WEIGHS ALL INFORMATION BEFORE DECIDING AN ANSWER -- **DEFERS JUDGMENT**
INTUITIVELY SEES ANSWERS WITHOUT INTERMEDIATE STEPS	DISPLAYS LONG ATTENTION SPAN -- WORKS EXERCISE DILIGENTLY TO THE END
PETS classwork indicates an outstanding ability to use this thinking skill.	The following student/s did not participate during the thinking skills lessons, but I see these behaviors during regular class time.

CONVERGENT THINKING
WHOLE CLASS
LESSON 1

PURPOSE

The purpose of this lesson is to reinforce the concepts of deductive logic and to introduce students to a logic grid which they can use to organize clues into a visual representation of a logic problem.

MATERIALS

— a copy of the story *Favorite Games*
— an overhead transparency marker
— an overhead transparency of *Favorite Games Logic Elimination Grid*
— an overhead transparency of *A Picnic in Crystal Pond Woods*
— an overhead transparency of *The Surprise Party*
— a duplicated class set of *Party Tales*
— a duplicated class set of *Party Favors*
— a duplicated class set of *Party Clean-Up*
— *PETS™ Behavioral Checklist - Convergent Thinking*

LESSON PLAN

1. If students have completed **PRIMARY EDUCATION THINKING SKILLS I,** they learned about *detective thinking*. The main points of detective thinking are listed below and should be reviewed. At this level, the term *deductive logic* will be used instead of detective thinking, and if this is the first time students have been introduced to deductive logic, the following points need to be made:

— There is one and only one right answer.
— Students may need to put together many pieces of information in order to find the one right answer.
— Students may feel like saying *"I have it!"* when they find the answer.
— Students may not see the answer right away and need to reflect on some of the clues.
— Patience is important to avoid jumping to incorrect conclusions.

2. Read the story *Favorite Games* aloud to students. These are the main points of the story:

— Logic grids are comprised of vertical columns and horizontal rows.
— The columns and rows criss-cross to create cells.
— These cells make a logic grid on which to organize information from the clues.

— Each column and row is labeled with information from the puzzle.
— The cells are marked with **X**'s and **O**'s.
— An **X** means that a pair of items **do not** go together.
— An **O** means that a pair of items **do** go together.
— To mark an appropriate cell, line up the correct column with the correct row, and find the cell where these intersect.
— Clues that do not make sense right away need to be pondered until they do make sense in the puzzle.
— When the puzzle is finished, each row and each column should have exactly one **O**.
— The result of the grid shows the one correct answer to the question posed by the logic puzzle.

3. Some students may be able to determine the correct answer without seeming to use the intermediate steps. Although this should be noted on the *PETS™ Behavioral Checklist - Convergent Thinking*, it is important for the teacher to continue the lesson so all students can observe how to complete a logic grid.

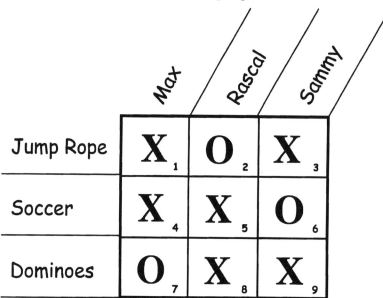

4. As a class activity, practice the logic grid process by completing *A Picnic in Crystal Pond Woods* and *The Surprise Party* on the overhead transparencies. (For convenience, the teacher may want to write the answers to the logic puzzles on a small piece of masking tape and attach it to the edge of the transparencies.)

Answer Keys:

A Picnic in Crystal Pond Woods
    Mike - Melissa
    Matt - Mary
    Mark - Michelle

The Surprise Party
    Dudley - punch
    Max - decorations
    Isabel - cups
    Jordan - cake

CHALLENGE PAGES

Party Tales
Party Favors
Party Clean-Up

5. *Party Tales* is a 3x3 logic puzzle and easier than *Party Favors*, a 4x4 logic puzzle. *Party Clean-Up*, a 5x5 logic puzzle, is the most difficult. Read clues to students if necessary, but do not help students with the deductive thinking process.

Answer Keys:

Party Tales
Max - Aladdin
Isabel - Little Mermaid
Jordan - Lion King

Party Favors
Dudley - fudge
Isabel - marshmallow
Jordan - vanilla creme
Max - peanut butter

Party Clean-Up
Dudley - recycle the cans
Isabel - sweep the floor
Jordan - take down balloons
Max - put away food
Sybil - wash the dishes

DIAGNOSTIC NOTES

During this lesson, the teacher and observer will be looking for students who display specific characteristics. These students may then be invited to the small group sessions for additional activities. Some teachers explain the structure of the **Primary Education Thinking Skills** curriculum to the students before actually starting the lessons. During the explanation, the teacher might point out to students the importance of volunteering during the lessons as this is the main opportunity for the teachers to observe what the students are thinking.

Characteristic behaviors and responses to look for in students are listed on the *PETS™ Behavioral Checklist - Convergent Thinking*. There is an overlap of characteristics between the units and certain traits will show up throughout the curriculum. The following is a short summary of what to look for in student behaviors and responses for Convergent Thinking Unit, Whole Class 1:

GRASPS CONCEPTS QUICKLY - Look for students who are quickly able to understand and to use the process of elimination. List the students who are the first to figure out the correct answers.

RECOGNIZES FLAWED REASONING - Look for students who are able to point out errors in logic.

INTUITIVELY SEES CORRECT ANSWERS - Some students who are excellent deductive thinkers are unable to verbalize how they figured out the answer. Note students who arrive at the correct conclusions without seeming to use the intermediate steps.

SEES AN INTERRELATIONSHIP OF CLUES - Look for students who are able to combine information from various clues in order to determine a correct solution.

ABLE TO DEFER JUDGMENT - Look for students who are willing to wait until they have gathered enough information to figure out the correct answer. These students avoid guessing impulsively.

DISPLAYS A LONG ATTENTION SPAN - Look for students who work diligently throughout the activity. In addition to a long attention span, look for students who want to work on convergent-type activities. An enthusiasm towards this type of problem usually indicates an ability to solve the problems.

Party Tales, Party Favors and *Party Clean-Up*

Most important in the identification portion of this lesson will be those students who are able to complete these Challenge Pages correctly and independently. Note these students in the appropriate box at the bottom of the *PETS™ Behavioral Checklist - Convergent Thinking.*

NOTES

FAVORITE GAMES

One day, Sybil the Scientist and Dudley the Detective were walking through Crystal Pond Woods. They had been discussing the latest mystery Dudley the Detective had solved. "You know, Dudley," said Sybil, "I am fascinated by how quickly you can put clues together and come up with the right answer to mysteries. How are you able to do that?"

"Well," Dudley replied modestly, "I often need to use a system for organizing my clues so that I can see the right answer quickly but logically."

"A system?" Sybil exclaimed. "Would you teach me your system?"

"Of course, I would," Dudley answered. He took a stick and drew a grid in the dirt.

*(Put the **Favorite Games Logic Elimination Grid** on the overhead.)*

"That looks like a windowpane or a tic-tac-toe board," said Sybil. "Are we going to play tic-tac-toe?"

"No," replied Dudley. "This special system is called a **logic elimination grid**. We will use **X**'s and **O**'s to organize our information from the clues. The boxes that go across are called rows. *(Demonstrate or highlight the rows of the grid on the overhead.)* Each row has a label. Suppose our mystery is to find out who in Crystal Pond Woods likes what game best. First we would label each row with a game that we know is popular in Crystal Pond Woods like this:

"Someone we know likes to jump rope, so we label one of our rows **jump rope**. *(Demonstrate.)* Someone else likes to play **soccer**, so that goes on the next row. *(Label accordingly.)* And another one of our friends likes to play **dominoes**, so that's the third label.

"Now, the boxes that go up and down are called columns. *(Demonstrate or highlight the columns of the grid.)* The columns need labels, too. We will label them with the names of our friends who like

these games. Since we know that one of these games is the favorite of Max the Magician, one is Rascal Racoon's favorite, and one of them is Sammy Squirrel's favorite, we will label the columns **Max**, **Rascal**, and **Sammy**. *(Demonstrate.)*

"The way the rows and columns criss-cross makes each little box, or cell, belong to a row and a column at the same time. We will use **X**'s to mean NO, WRONG, or NOT A MATCH. We will use **O**'s when we find a pair that IS a match."

"I think I'm beginning to see," said Sybil, "but I don't get how the **X**'s and **O**'s are used."

"That's because we haven't looked at the clues yet," assured Dudley. "Suppose I told you that Max's top hat gets knocked off every time he tries to jump rope?"

"Then he probably wouldn't like jumping rope very much!" cried Sybil. "And it certainly wouldn't be his favorite game!"

"That's right," agreed Dudley. "So we mark that information on the grid like this: I'll take Max's column and the row marked jump rope and pull my fingers together until they meet. *(Point at Max's column with one finger and point at jump rope with the other hand to demonstrate.)* This is the cell that belongs to both Max and the jump rope. Since we know this is not Max's favorite game, this cell gets an **X** to show that there's no match." *(Place an **X** in cell 1.)*

"I get it!" cried Sybil. "This is easy!"

"Now what if I said that Sammy's favorite game starts with the same letter as his name?" asked Dudley.

"That would be soccer!" exclaimed Sybil. "You should line up Sammy with soccer and mark that cell!"

Dudley did as Sybil suggested, following Sammy's column down and the soccer row across until his fingers met. *(Demonstrate.)* "What kind of mark should I put here? An **X**?"

"No," said Sybil, "because Sammy DOES like soccer best. It's a match, so you should mark that cell with an **O**."

"That's right," said Dudley, as he placed an **O** in the cell. *(Place an O in cell 6.)* "Now, there's something else to remember. Since we know that Sammy's favorite game is soccer, he will not have any other favorite games - - this is very important! So I will put an **X** in each of Sammy's other cells, because I know he won't like to jump rope best *(put an X in cell 3)* and he won't like dominoes best *(put an X in cell 9)*. And since Sammy's favorite game is soccer, that means it can't be Rascal's or Max's favorite game." *(Put an X in cell 4 and in cell 5.)*

"Now look!" cried Sybil. "Max only has one cell left open in his column since you eliminated all the others! His favorite game <u>must</u> be dominoes!"

"That's right," approved Dudley. "Since I told you that each one of our friends must have a favorite game, each of them <u>must</u> have an **O** in his column. Since all of Max's column is **X**'d out except that one cell, it must be the cell showing his favorite game." Dudley placed an **O** in the cell where Max and dominoes line up. *(Place an O in cell 7.)*

"And since Max likes dominoes best," reasoned Sybil, "then I know that Rascal won't, so I'll put an **X** where Rascal's column lines up with dominoes." Sybil took the stick from Dudley and made an **X**. *(Put an X in cell 8.)* "Now, since the only cell left open for Rascal is jump rope, I'll put an **O** there, and we've solved the mystery!"

"That's how it's done," smiled Dudley the Detective proudly. "Do you think you could do a mystery all by yourself now using logical thinking and a logic elimination grid?"

Do you?

Favorite Games
Logic Elimination
Grid

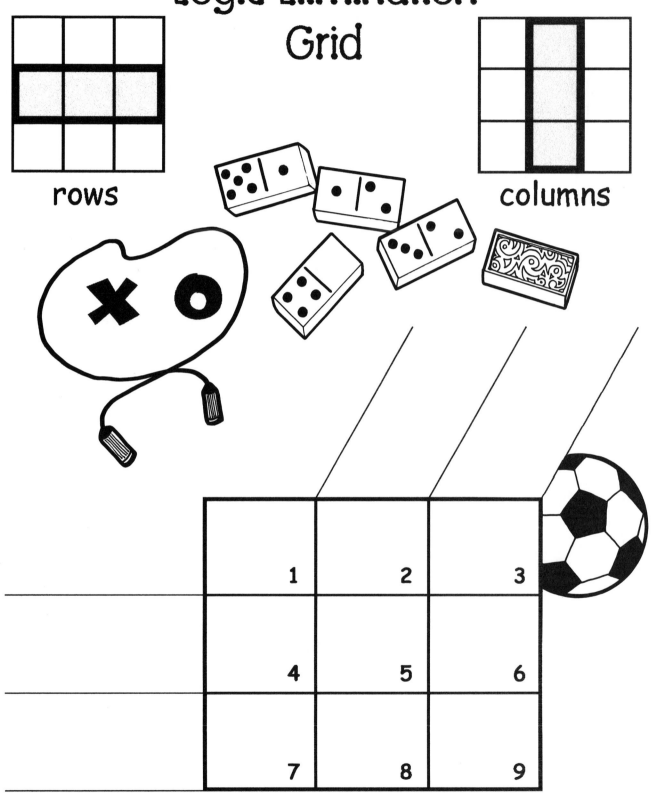

rows

columns

	1	2	3
	4	5	6
	7	8	9

A Picnic in Crystal Pond Woods

Children often come to play in Crystal Pond Woods. One day the woods is visited by 6 children having a picnic. These 6 children are Mike, Matt, Mark, Mary, Michelle, and Melissa. Each boy in the group has one sister in the group, and each girl has one brother in the group. No two girls have the same brother, and no two boys have the same sister. See if you can unravel the clues to match brother and sister pairs. Use the elimination process.

1. Mike and Michelle did not know one another before today.
2. Matt and Mary have the same last name.

	Mary	Michelle	Melissa
Mike	1	2	3
Matt	4	5	6
Mark	7	8	9

The Surprise Party

Sybil decided to throw a surprise party for her friend, Yolanda. She invited 4 friends and asked each of them to bring something to help her with the party.

Read all the clues below. Find out how each friend helped Sybil with her surprise party. Finish labeling the grid. Then use the elimination process.

1. Max brought the decorations.
2. Dudley did not bring the cups for the punch.
3. Isabel does not like to cook, but she did bring something.
4. Jordan baked the cake.

	decorations			
Dudley	1	2	3	4
	5	6	7	8
	9	10	11	12
	13	14	15	16

Name _____

Party Tales

Yolanda the Yarnspinner's friends really enjoy listening to her tell stories.

At Yolanda's party, Isabel, Max, and Jordan each asked Yolanda to tell one of their favorite fairy tales. To find out who asked Yolanda to tell which story, read the clues below.

1. Isabel's story did **not** have any monkeys in it.
2. The title of Max's story did **not** have three words in it.

	Max	Isabel	Jordan
The Lion King	1	2	3
Aladdin	4	5	6
The Little Mermaid	7	8	9

Name _____

Party Favors

At Yolanda's surprise birthday party, Sybil gave each of her friends a party favor. Each guest received his or her favorite candy! Read all the clues. Then put the clues together to find out which guest received which candy. Each guest has a different favorite candy.

1. Dudley likes fudge best.
2. Isabel ate a candy that was white inside.
3. Jordan does not like any kind of nuts.
4. Max likes the kind of candy that Jordan does not.
5. Jordan's favorite candy flavor is the same as his favorite ice cream flavor.

	fudge	vanilla creme	peanut cluster	marshmallow
Dudley	1	2	3	4
Isabel	5	6	7	8
Jordan	9	10	11	12
Max	13	14	15	16

Name _____

Party Clean-Up

Following Yolanda's surprise birthday party, everyone offered to help Sybil clean up. Read all the clues. How did each friend help Sybil ?

1. Sybil used soap and water to do her job.
2. Dudley did not sweep.
3. Jordan needed a ladder to do his job.
4. Isabel had a job.
5. Max needed to ask Sybil where she kept the plastic wrap for leftovers.

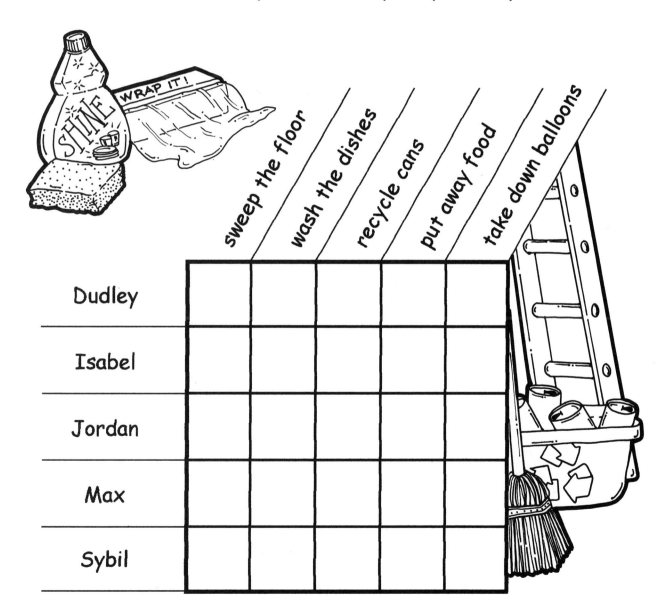

	sweep the floor	wash the dishes	recycle cans	put away food	take down balloons
Dudley					
Isabel					
Jordan					
Max					
Sybil					

CONVERGENT THINKING
WHOLE CLASS
LESSON 2

PURPOSE

The purpose of this lesson is to introduce and reinforce the concepts of analytical thinking through the use of Venn diagrams.

MATERIALS

- — a copy of the story *Dudley's Blocks*
- — three plastic coffee can lid circles or 3 copies of the overhead transparency *Sybil's Circles*
- — an overhead transparency set of *Dudley's Attribute Blocks* or a commercial set of overhead attribute blocks
- — a duplicated class set of *Sybil's Collection of Sortable Shapes*
- — a duplicated class set of *Sortable Shapes 1*
- — a duplicated class set of *Sortable Shapes 2*
- — *PETS™ Behavioral Checklist - Convergent Thinking*

LESSON PLAN

1. If students completed **PRIMARY EDUCATION THINKING SKILLS I,** they learned that scientists classify and organize information. At this level *thinking like a scientist* is called analytical thinking. In this lesson, students will be using Venn diagrams to practice *analytical thinking*.

2. If the overhead transparency set of *Dudley's Attribute Blocks* is used instead of commercial overhead attribute blocks, color the blocks prior to the lesson. Use red, blue and yellow. Color one large rectangle red, another large rectangle blue and the last large rectangle yellow. Follow this pattern for all of the shapes.

3. Using coffee can lid circles for the Venn diagrams may be preferable to using the overhead transparency provided because the coffee can lid circles will pull the blocks as they are moved on the overhead projector. To make a plastic circle, cut away the inside part of a coffee can lid as well as the rim, leaving the raised ring. Each plastic ring will need to be colored with a different colored marker. If the overhead transparencies are used as the circles for the Venn diagrams, cut out the circles and color them in different colors.

4. Read the story *Dudley's Blocks* aloud to students. These are the main points of the story:

— Each circle of a Venn diagram contains items of a like attribute.
— The intersection of the Venn circles contains items that share attributes from <u>both</u> circles.
— Analyzing the attributes of items helps to classify them into categories that can be represented on a Venn diagram.

CHALLENGE PAGES

Sybil's Collection of Sortable Shapes
Sortable Shapes 1
Sortable Shapes 2

5. Distribute the Challenge Pages to the students. *Sybil's Collection of Sortable Shapes* has two sets of the shapes; one is used for *Sortable Shapes 1* and the other is used for *Sortable Shapes 2*. If students are going to do both Challenge Pages at the same time, the teacher may want to copy *Sybil's Collection of Sortable Shapes* so that each student has a different color set for *Sortable Shapes 1* than for *Sortable Shapes 2*. Students are to determine a label for each Venn diagram and place the shapes in the Venn diagrams using as many shapes as possible. Students may need to test various labels before deciding on the two or three which provide areas for the most blocks. Answers will vary.

DIAGNOSTIC NOTES

The following is a short summary of what to look for in student behaviors and responses for Convergent Thinking, Whole Class 2:

GRASPS CONCEPTS QUICKLY - Look for students who quickly and easily see discrete sets (sets with no overlap).

RECOGNIZES FLAWED REASONING - Look for students who foresee when certain attributes will not work in the Venn diagram structure without manipulating the shapes or using trial and error. Look for students who point out errors in the reasoning of others.

INTUITIVELY SEES ANSWERS - Some students are able to see intuitively the way items fit into the intersecting areas of the Venn diagram. Note these students.

SEES AN INTERRELATIONSHIP OF CLUES - Look for students who see how to build one clue's information on a previous clue to fit the pieces.

ABLE TO DEFER JUDGMENT - Look for students who are willing to wait until they have thought through the puzzle before determining the attributes of the rings. These students avoid impulsive guessing.

DISPLAYS A LONG ATTENTION SPAN - Look for students who work diligently throughout the activity. In addition to a long attention span, look for students who want to work on convergent-type activities. An enthusiasm towards this type of problem may indicate an ability to solve the problems.

Sortable Shapes 1 and *2*

Also important in the identification portion of this lesson will be those students who are able to complete these Challenge Pages correctly and independently. Note these students in the appropriate box at the bottom of the *PETS™ Behavioral Checklist - Convergent Thinking.*

NOTES

DUDLEY'S BLOCKS

As usual on Saturdays, Sybil the Scientist went to play with her friend Dudley the Detective. She found him on this particular Saturday staring at a collection of blocks. "What are you doing?" she asked him.

Dudley looked up, still wearing his look of concentration. "I want to organize these old blocks of mine," he told her. "It always looks so easy when you classify things in your lab, but I have no idea how you do it. Will you teach me?"

"Of course," said Sybil. "It's really quite simple." Sybil sat down next to Dudley. "First, we just need to look closely at the blocks."

"What are we looking for?" Dudley asked.

"Attributes," Sybil replied.

"Attri-*what*?" Dudley asked.

"Attributes," Sybil repeated. "Those are special characteristics that everything in the world has. Some things have one kind of characteristic, while other things have different characteristics. Attributes are what make things what they are. For instance, the fact that these are all one set of blocks automatically gives them at least one attribute in common: they are all made of the same material."

"But if they are all made of the same thing, how does that help us organize them?" Dudley asked.

"**That** doesn't," Sybil agreed, "because they all have that characteristic in common. In order to organize them into smaller groups, we need to look for characteristics that **some** of your blocks have, but others do not."

"You mean like some of the blocks are big and some are small?"

"Exactly," smiled Sybil. "We could make two groups." Sybil made two circles out of yarn and laid them on Dudley's table. *(Demonstrate on the overhead projector by laying two plastic circles side by side.)* "We could put all the small blocks in the circle on the left and all the big blocks in the circle on the right. **Big** and **little** would be a characteristic or attribute of your blocks. They have other attributes, too."

"Shapes," replied Dudley instantly. "I like them because of their different shapes."

"OK," said Sybil. "We can organize them by shapes, too. Let's keep all the little blocks in the circle on the left, but now let's put all the square blocks in the circle on the right."

"This sounds like fun," said Dudley. "Are you sure we're **classifying**, the way you do in your scientific lab?"

"Exactly the way I do in my lab," Sybil assured him. Sybil laid the big blue square in the circle on the right. *(Demonstrate by laying the big blue square in the circle on the right.)* "See?" she said. "This square goes here because the circle on the right is for squares."

Dudley laid the big yellow square in the right circle, too. "This is like a fun game," he said, "but one thing puzzles me. What should I do with **this** square?" In his hand, Dudley held up a small blue square. *(Show the class this square.)* "It should go in the circle on the right, because it is a square, but it is also small, so I think it could go in the circle on the left, too."

"Good point, Dudley!" Sybil replied. "It **could** go in both groups, so for that block we need something special." Sybil reached out and drew the two circles together until they overlapped in the middle. *(Demonstrate with the plastic circles.)* "Now there is a space in the middle that is actually part of **both** circles," Sybil pointed out. "Your small blue square can go in there. That way it will be in the circle for square blocks **and** the circle for small blocks."

"This is great!" cried Dudley. "I like classifying!"

"I knew you would," Sybil smiled at her friend. "Now I'm really going to try to stump you. What if I make a third circle for red blocks?" Sybil laid a **third** circle overlapping the other two in the center. *(Demonstrate with the circles.)* "If this circle is for red blocks, where will you put this big red triangle?"

(The story may be continued at this point or students can instruct the teacher where to put other attribute blocks. Be sure to include blocks for each area of the overlapping circles so students clearly see what each area represents.)

"The big red triangle should go in the outer section of the third circle," said Dudley, "because it is red, but it is not small nor is it square."

"Very good!" said Sybil. "What about this small red hexagon?"

"That will go in the section where the circle for red blocks overlaps the circle for small blocks, but we would not include it in the circle for squares," answered Dudley.

Sybil the Scientist complimented Dudley the Detective, "You're really good at this! What do you think we should do with this small yellow square?"

Dudley the Detective quickly placed it in the section where the "small" circle overlapped the "square" circle. He added the small blue square to the same section. Then Dudley the Detective reached into the pile of blocks. "I even know what goes in the very center section," he said. He carefully placed the small red square in the center. "This block fits all three groups," he said proudly. "I"ve got it!" Sybil the Scientist smiled at her friend because she had shown Dudley the Detective a new way to have fun.

Sybil's Circles

Use three of Sybil's circles to solve the puzzles in *Dudley's Blocks*.

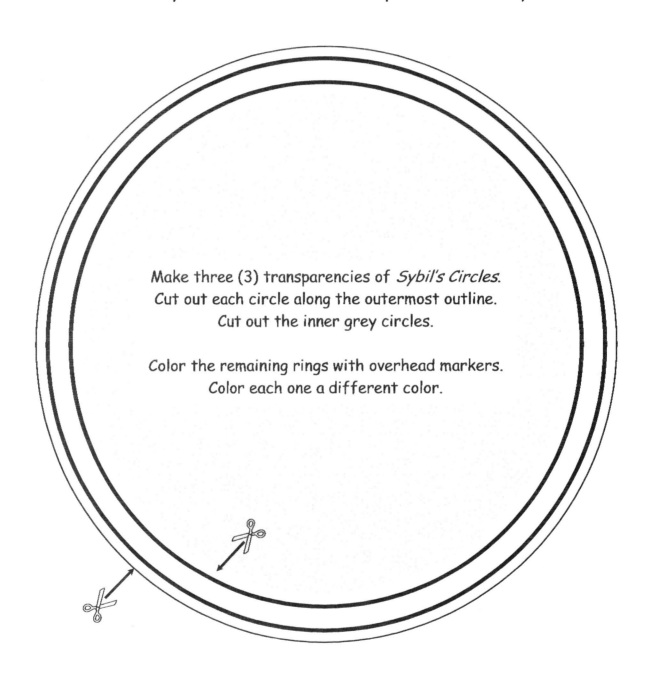

Make three (3) transparencies of *Sybil's Circles*.
Cut out each circle along the outermost outline.
Cut out the inner grey circles.

Color the remaining rings with overhead markers.
Color each one a different color.

Dudley's Attribute Blocks

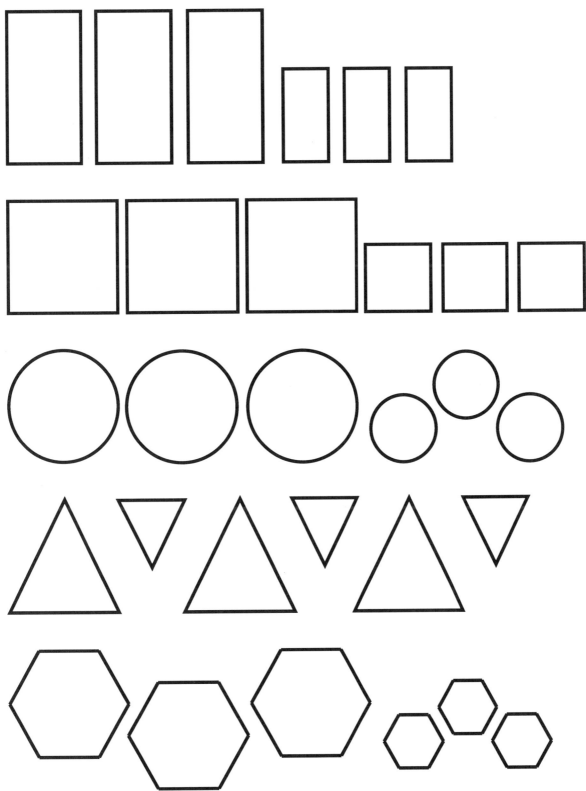

Sybil's Collection of Sortable Shapes

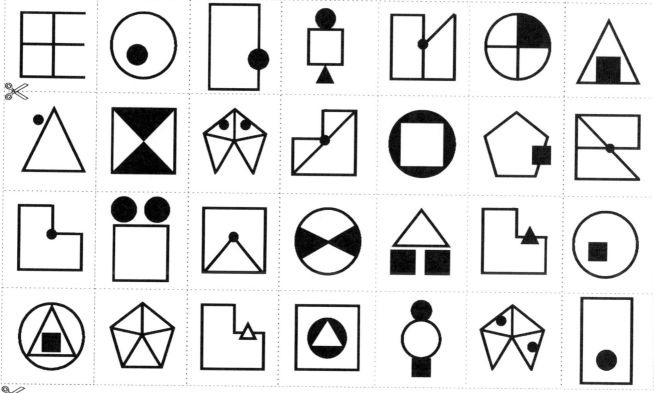

Sybil's Collection of Sortable Shapes

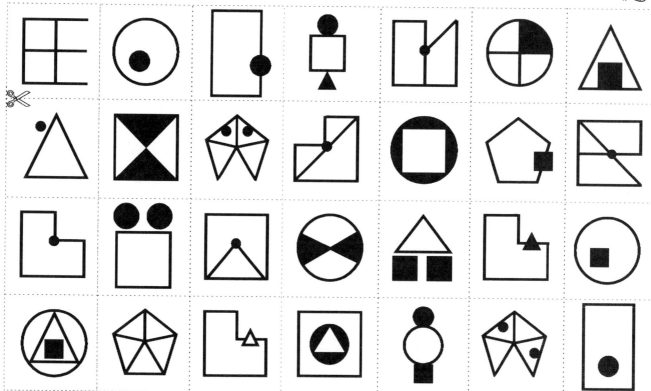

Name_____

Sortable Shapes 1

Help Sybil the Scientist organize her collection of shapes in this pair of Sybil's Circles.
Be sure to put at least one shape in each space. Place as many of the shapes as you can.
Label each circle.

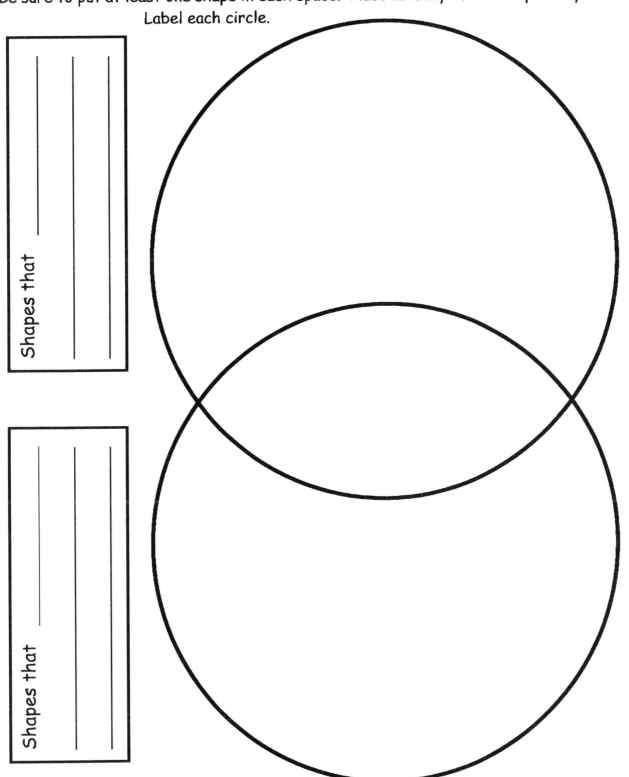

Shapes that _____

Shapes that _____

Sortable Shapes 2

Help Sybil the Scientist organize her collection of shapes in this set of Sybil's Circles.
Be sure to put at least one shape in each space. Place as many of the shapes as you can.
Label each circle.

Shapes that _____
_____
_____

Shapes that _____
_____
_____

Shapes that _____
_____
_____

CONVERGENT THINKING
WHOLE CLASS
LESSON 3

PURPOSE

PURPOSE

The purpose of this lesson is to reinforce the concepts of convergent thinking by combining the deductive reasoning of Dudley the Detective with the analysis of Sybil the Scientist.

MATERIALS

— a copy of the story *Fall Cleaning in Sybil's Lab*
— an overhead transparency marker
— an overhead transparency of *Sybil's Containers*
— an overhead transparency of *Sybil's Shelf*
— a duplicated class set of *Crazy Collections*
— a duplicated class set of *Private Properties*
— *PETS™ Behavioral Checklist - Convergent Thinking*

LESSON PLAN

1. If students have completed PETS 1, they have learned about *thinking like a detective* and *thinking like a scientist*. At this level, introduce the term *convergent thinking* to students. Convergent thinking incorporates characteristics of both deductive logic and analytical thinking. Good convergent thinkers study the component parts to arrive at the correct answer.

2. This lesson combines the convergent thinking skills of Dudley the Detective and Sybil the Scientist. Read the story *Fall Cleaning in Sybil's Lab* aloud to students. During the reading of the story, the students will use analytical thinking skills to label the containers correctly and use deductive logic skills to figure out the correct order in which the containers should be arranged on the shelf.

3. During the reading of the story, students may come up with workable labels that differ from those labels used in the story. Use the student-generated labels and adjust the story as needed.

CHALLENGE PAGES   *Crazy Collections   Private Properties*

4. Distribute *Crazy Collections* and *Private Properties* to students. Read directions to students if necessary, but do not help students with the deductive or analytical thinking processes.

Some possible answers for *Crazy Collections* include:

Bag Label
same shape within a shape
black within white

Cup Label
things made of wood
things with straight edges

Jar Label
things you play with
things for free time

Box Label
animals that hibernate

There may be other possible solutions, and any answer that can be justified should be accepted.

Answers for *Private Properties*
    Max - jar
    Jordan - cup
    Dudley - bag
    Sybil - box

DIAGNOSTIC NOTES

The following is a short summary of what to look for in student behaviors and responses for Convergent Thinking, Whole Class 3:

GRASPS CONCEPTS QUICKLY - Look for students who accurately remember the processes of analysis and deduction presented in the first two lessons. Look for students who arrive at correct answers quickly.

RECOGNIZES FLAWED REASONING - Look for students who are able to point out errors in logic.

INTUITIVELY SEES ANSWERS - Look for students who arrive at the correct conclusions without seeming to use intermediary steps.

SEES AN INTERRELATIONSHIP OF CLUES - Listen carefully to student reasoning when labeling the containers, and note those students with creative yet substantiated answers. It is important not to place preconceived ideas of right answers on the labeling of the containers.

ABLE TO DEFER JUDGMENT - Look for students who are willing to wait until they have figured out the correct answer. These students avoid guessing until they determine the correct answer.

DISPLAYS A LONG ATTENTION SPAN - Look for students who work diligently throughout the activity. In addition to a long attention span, look for students who want to work on convergent-type activities. An enthusiasm towards this type of problem usually indicates an ability to solve the problems.

Crazy Collections and *Private Properties*

Most important in the identification portion of this lesson will be those students who are able to complete these Challenge Pages correctly and independently. Students need to be able to justify unexpected responses. Note these students in the appropriate box at the bottom of the *PETS™ Behavioral Checklist - Convergent Thinking.*

NOTES

FALL CLEANING IN SYBIL'S LAB

Late one afternoon, Dudley the Detective arrived at the laboratory of his friend Sybil the Scientist. He found Sybil wearing a big apron and a kerchief around her head instead of her usual white lab coat. "My goodness!" Dudley the Detective exclaimed. "What on earth are you doing?"

"Oh, I'm just finishing up my fall cleaning," explained Sybil. "Would you like to help?"

"Sure," Dudley replied. "What would you like me to do?"

"I'd appreciate it if you would label these containers for me and organize them on that high shelf over there," Sybil directed as she placed an armload of containers on the counter in front of Dudley. "I use these for storing specimens as I collect them," she explained. "Just label them according to what's inside them." Then Sybil went back to dusting in another part of the laboratory.

Dudley looked inside the first container. *(Place the basket from **Sybil's Containers** on the overhead projector.)* He saw that it contained a bunch of numbers. It was tagged on the outside with a big red circle that had a line through it. Dudley knew that circle. It was the international symbol for "**No.**" More numbers were listed on the tag. Dudley cleverly realized that Sybil did not want those numbers on the tag to be grouped with the numbers in the basket. Dudley tried to remember what Sybil had told him about analyzing the characteristics of things in order to help organize them. What did the numbers 22, 16, and 48 in the basket have in common that the numbers 17, 3, and 9 in the circle did not have? *(Ask students to volunteer their ideas at this point.)*

"That's it!" Dudley realized that only even numbers were in the basket. He proudly lettered E-V-E-N N-U-M-B-E-R-S on the label of the basket. *(Label the basket.)*

Dudley took a look at the paper bag next. *(Place the paper bag from **Sybil's Containers** on the overhead projector.)* Inside it were pants, pliers, and scissors. Its circle tag read *hammer* and *dress*. This was tougher. What did pants, pliers, and scissors have in common that made them different from a hammer and a dress? *(Again ask students to volunteer their ideas.)*

Pairs! Things that come in pairs! Dudley lettered P-A-I-R-S on the bag. *(Label the bag.)*

(Follow the same principle with the remaining three containers. The correct label for the can is "things that are opened." The label on the jar is "things whose names are also letters of the alphabet." The label on the box is "things that go up and down.")

When Dudley was finished labeling the containers, he took them to Sybil, who complimented him on his useful labels. "While you were working on that," said Sybil, "I made you a little puzzle like the ones you were teaching me the other day. I know how much you like mystery puzzles, so I thought you might find this a fun way to organize the containers on the shelf in the order I want them."

Dudley smiled and took the puzzle from Sybil. "Thanks, Sybil," he said. "I'm sure I can do the job for you."

*(Put **Sybil's Shelf** on the overhead projector and read through the clues with the students. As a class use the logic elimination process and its system of X's and O's presented in the first lesson of this unit to fill out the grid. Then arrange the containers on the overhead in the order Sybil wants them on her shelf. The correct order of the containers is: can, jar, basket, bag, box.)*

Dudley called Sybil over to admire his work. "Just perfect, Dudley!" Sybil the Scientist praised. "I'll remember you the next time I need to clean my shelves in here."

"Just make a fun mystery puzzle out of it," Dudley the Detective replied, "and I'll be glad to help any time!"

Sybil's Containers

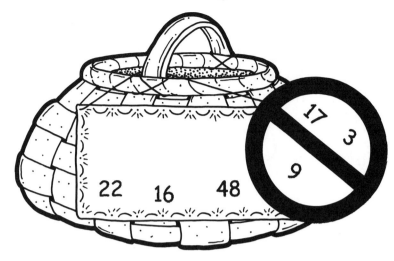

17 3
9
22   16   48

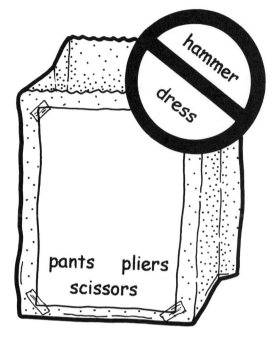

hammer
dress

pants   pliers
scissors

pennies
fork

book   umbrella
birthday present

ear
me

you   sea
eye

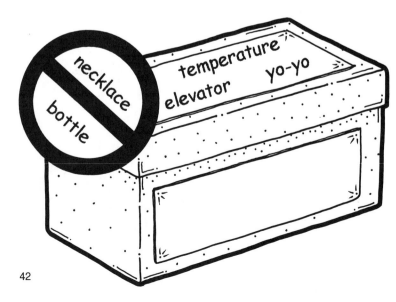

necklace
bottle

temperature   yo-yo
elevator

Sybil's Shelf

Help Dudley the Detective organize the containers on Sybil the Scientist's laboratory shelf. Read all the clues. Put the containers in the right order.

1. The jar is **not** first.
2. The bag is between the basket and the box.
3. The "B" containers are **not** at the beginning of the shelf.
4. The basket is in the middle.

	1st	2nd	3rd	4th	5th
Jar	1	2	3	4	5
Can	6	7	8	9	10
Box	11	12	13	14	15
Basket	16	17	18	19	20
Bag	21	22	23	24	25

Name_____

Crazy Collections

More unmarked containers have been found in Sybil the Scientist's lab! What should these crazy collections be labelled?

44

Private Properties

Dudley and Sybil really enjoy logic elimination puzzles. They decided to use a logic grid to help them determine which of the newly labelled collections belongs to which of their friends. Use the information from the clues to help label the columns and rows. Use X's, O's, and the logic elimination process to solve this puzzle.

1. As a magician, Max has more free time than his friends. He keeps his collection in a container with a removable lid.

2. Jordan collects items which remind him of his tree home. He keeps them in a rounded container.

3. One collection belongs to Sybil.

4. The bag of shapes are special coded symbols which Dudley uses in secret messages.

5. The box contains animals which do not belong to Max.

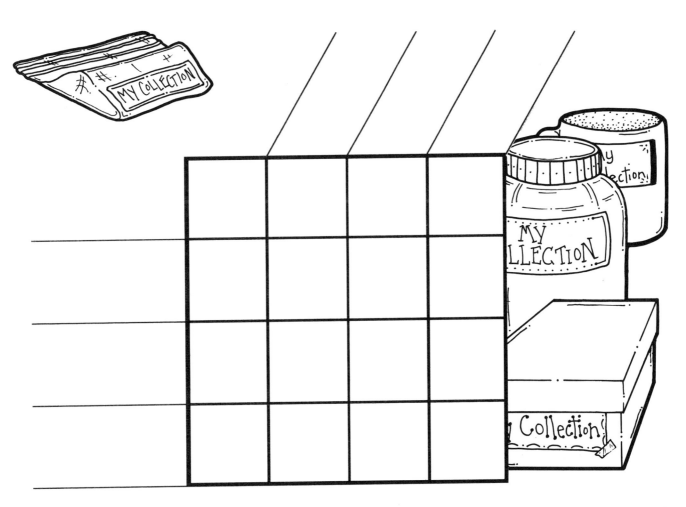

CONVERGENT THINKING
SMALL GROUP
LESSON 1

PURPOSE

The purpose of this lesson is to reinforce deductive thinking skills by using clues to arrive at the one correct answer.

MATERIALS

— a set of *PETS™ Silhouettes* for each student
— a duplicated class set of *PETS™ Silhouette Puzzles #1* and *#2, #3* and *#4,* and *#5* and *#6*
— a copy of *PETS™ Small Group Checklist* for each student

LESSON PLAN

1. As explained in the introduction, the *PETS™ Small Group Checklist* is used by the teacher to note additional behaviors that identify talented learners. A *PETS™ Small Group Checklist* is needed for each student in the small group lesson.

2. Cut out the *PETS™ Silhouettes* before starting the activity. Teachers may want to laminate them for use year after year.

3. Students will be using clues to determine the correct square on the *PETS™ Silhouettes* grid for each of the *PETS™ Silhouettes*. Use all nine clues on each puzzle card to find the correct places for the silhouettes. There is only one right solution for each puzzle card. Explain or demonstrate the following directions to students:

— If the box is shaded, it indicates the silhouette designated DOES go in that spot.
— If the designated silhouette has a line through it, similar to the international "no" symbol, then that silhouette does NOT go in the shaded space.
— If only a shape is shown, then one of the silhouettes of that shape goes in the shaded square, but the students may have to wait to determine which one.
— If more than one square is shaded for a particular clue, then the students have to choose (by using some of the other clues) which shaded square is the correct spot for the silhouette in question.
— If there is a selection of boxes and the designated silhouette has a line through it, then that silhouette will not go in ANY of the shaded squares.
— If there is already a silhouette shown in place on one of the clues, that silhouette's location must be determined before the designated silhouette can be established. Knowing the placement of the first silhouette is part of the clue to where the other silhouette goes.

— In Puzzles #3-6, the entire grid is not always shown. The students must determine which portion of the grid is shown. For example, a row of three boxes might be the top row, middle row or bottom row of the grid.

4. The puzzles are numbered in order of difficulty. Have students work through the puzzles sequentially. *Puzzle #1* is very easy and gives students an opportunity to learn the silhouette characters and how to place them on the grid. An answer key is provided to check student work.

PETS Silhouette Puzzle Solutions

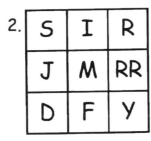
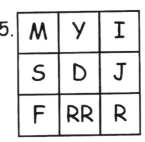

1.
M	S	F
I	D	RR
J	R	Y

2.
S	I	R
J	M	RR
D	F	Y

3.
RR	S	M
I	D	Y
J	R	F

4.
Y	S	R
J	F	M
RR	D	I

5.
M	Y	I
S	D	J
F	RR	R

6.
I	F	D
M	J	Y
R	RR	S

KEY

D	Dudley the Detective
I	Isabel the Inventor
J	Jordan the Judge
M	Max the Magician
S	Sybil the Scientist
Y	Yolanda the Yarnspinner
F	Felix Fish
R	Rascal Raccoon
RR	Rosalyn Robin

DIAGNOSTIC NOTES

Look for students who can quickly and accurately interpret the clues and arrive at the correct solution. Some students will carefully work through the clues and manipulate the silhouettes as they think through the process. Being able to combine clues to arrive at the correct solution is important.

Look for students who are able to ponder clues which do not give enough information at first but are useful later. However, keep in mind that other students may place their silhouettes immediately onto the right squares, skipping any intermediary steps. Both types of thinkers show talent in this area.

PETS Silhouettes

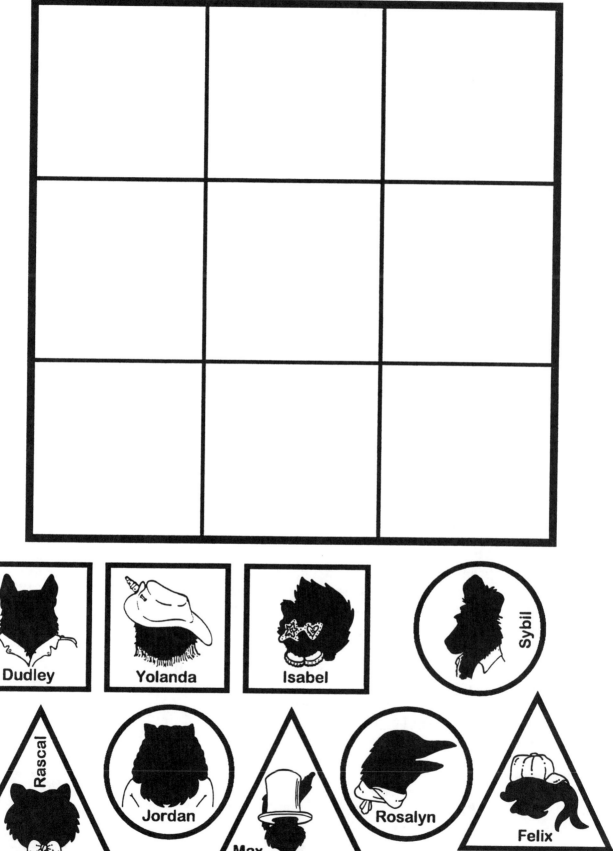

Dudley

Yolanda

Isabel

Sybil

Rascal

Jordan

Max

Rosalyn

Felix

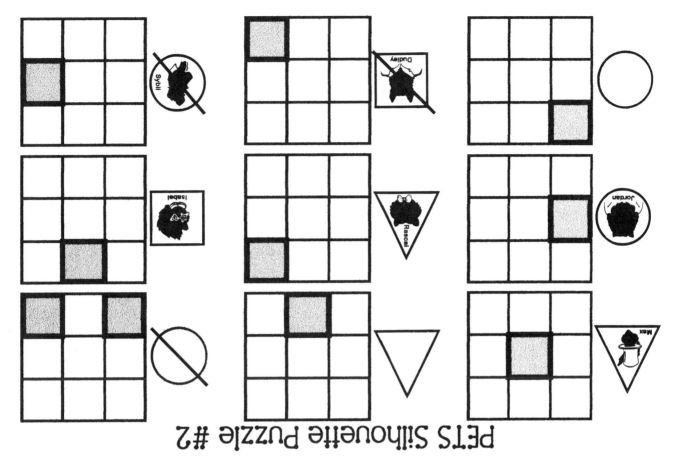

PETS Silhouette Puzzle #2

Fold or cut ———

PETS Silhouette Puzzle #1

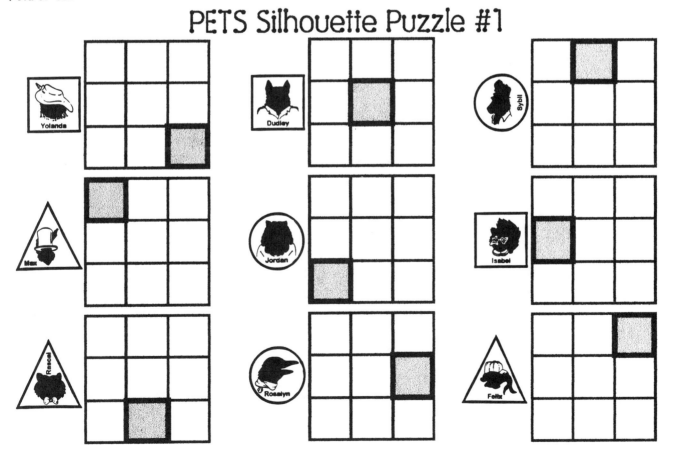

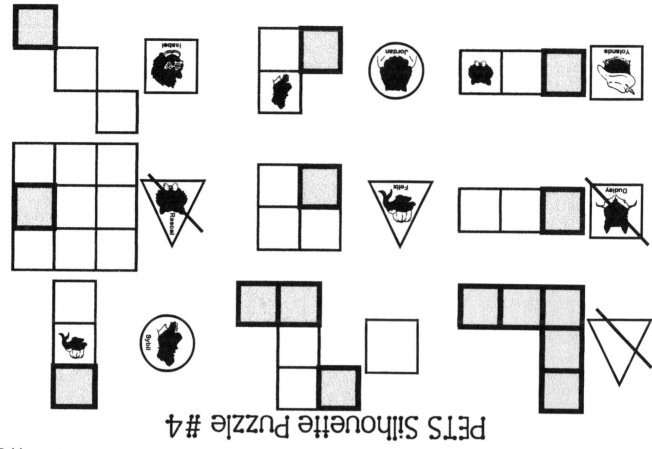

PETS Silhouette Puzzle #4

Fold or cut —

PETS Silhouette Puzzle #3

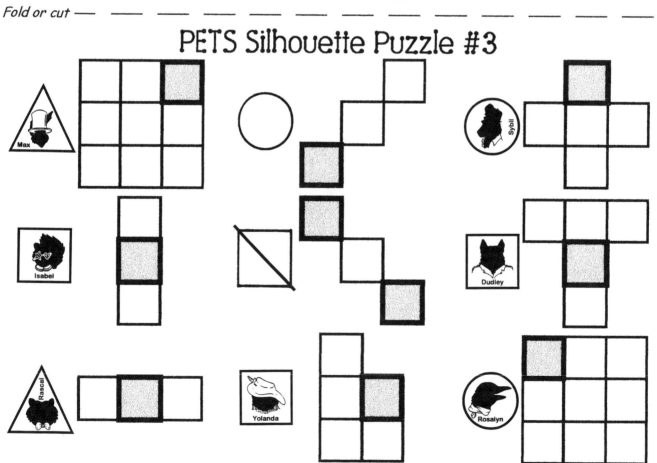

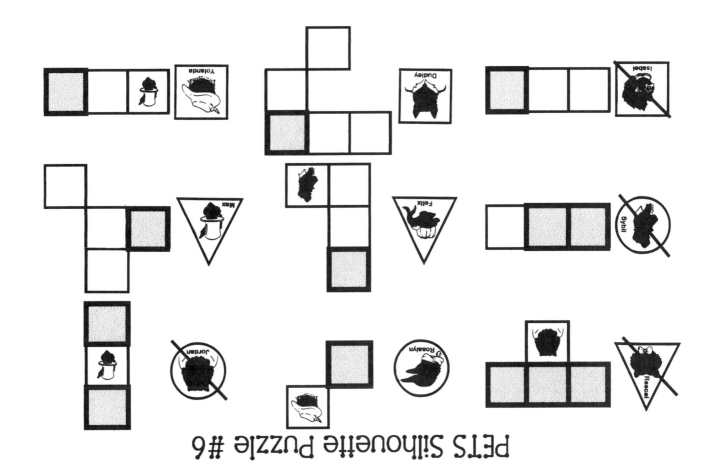

PETS Silhouette Puzzle #6

Fold or cut ————————————————————————

PETS Silhouette Puzzle #5

CONVERGENT THINKING
SMALL GROUP
LESSON 2

PURPOSE

The purpose of this lesson is to give students an opportunity to practice convergent analytical thinking by identifying attributes found in the shapes on the *Attribute Stax*™ cards.

MATERIALS

— one 60-card deck of *Attribute Stax™*
— a four-sided die or a cube die with "5" and "6" covered with masking tape
— a copy of *PETS™ Small Group Checklist* for each student

LESSON PLAN

1. *Attribute Stax™* is a game played using a set of 60 cards with a variety of shapes and colors. In order for the cards to possess the attribute of COLOR, make copies of each *Attribute Stax™* blackline master on three different colors of paper or card stock. As an option, each blackline master can be copied three times and then each two-page set colored a different color. Teachers may want to laminate the cards for use year after year.

2. The shapes on the *Attribute Stax™* share the following attributes:
   SHAPE— square, oval, star, triangle, pentagon
   COLOR— for example: yellow, green, pink
   SIZE— large or small
   HOLES OR NO HOLES
Shapes may be different from each other in one, two, three, or four ways. A **large, green star with no hole** is different in one and only one way (size) from a **small, green star with no hole**. The same **large, green star with no hole** is different in two ways from a **large, yellow square with no hole**. The differences are color and shape. A **large, green square with no hole** is different in three ways from a **small, green star with a hole.** The differences are size, hole or no hole, and shape. Finally a **large, pink oval with a hole** is different in four ways from a **small, yellow triangle with no hole.** The two shapes differ in every attribute.

3. The teacher begins the game by rolling a die numbered 1 through 4. This will decide whether the shapes in this hand of *Attribute Stax™* should be different in one, two, three or four ways as cards are played.

4. Deal six cards to each student. In order for the teacher to assess student reasoning, all students should play the game with their cards face up on the table. The remainder of the deck is placed face down in the center of the table. This will be the "draw pile." The top card is turned over and becomes the "target card."

5. Play goes left to right, beginning with whomever has the most large shapes dealt to him or her. The first player studies the "target card" and places a card from his or her hand on top of it. This card is to be different in one, two, three or four ways, as determined by the die. The next player now sees a new "target card" and must lay a card on top that is different in the number of ways determined by the die at the beginning of the game. Each played card becomes the new "target card" for the next player.

6. If a player does not have a card in his or her hand that is different in the required number of ways, one card must be drawn from the "draw pile." If the drawn card can be played, the player may do so during this turn. Otherwise the card is added to the student's hand.

7. The placing of a card may be challenged. If the player has made a mistake, he or she loses that turn and must take a card from the "draw pile." If the challenger is in error, the challenger must take a card from the "draw pile." The teacher should monitor challenges for accuracy. Playing the game *with* students provides a way to do this.

8. The game may end when one of the players has placed all of his or her cards on the "target pile." However the teacher may choose to continue play until all the students have had a chance to go out in order to observe other students' strategies.

DIAGNOSTIC NOTES

Look for students who recognize and use attribute differences in a strategy to win *Attribute Stax™*.

"Table conversation" can be very diagnostic as students are playing the game.

Note students who are able to recognize moves in other students' hands. Some students may show the ability to anticipate future moves by opponents, forcing them to draw a card. Figuring out a strategy and consistently winning indicates a student with high potential.

Attribute Stax™

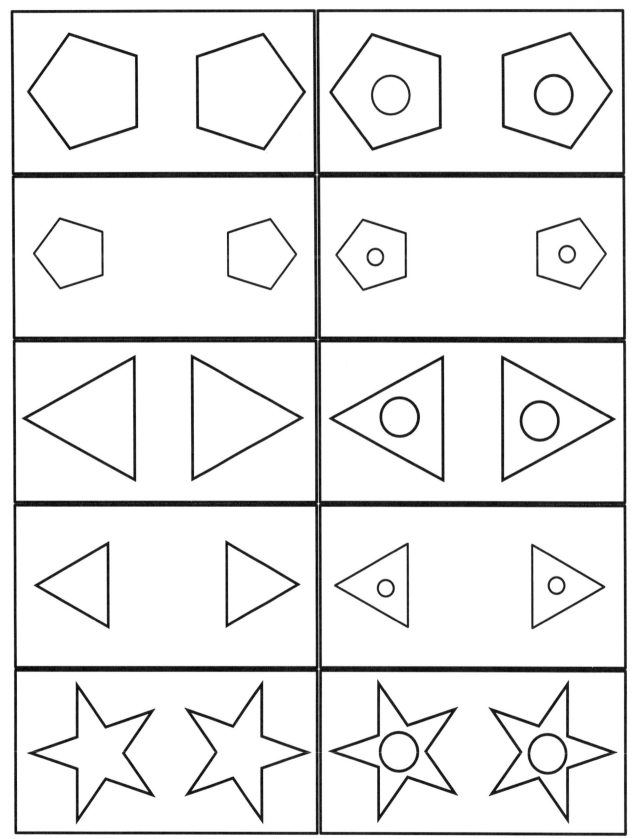

Attribute Stax™

CONVERGENT THINKING
SMALL GROUP
LESSON 3

PURPOSE

The purpose of this lesson is to give students an opportunity to practice convergent deductive thinking skills to arrive at a correct answer.

MATERIALS

— one copy of *Dinner At Max's* puzzle and table for each group
— one copy of *Yolanda's Literary Circle* puzzle and table for each group
— one copy of *Jordan's Luncheon Party* puzzle and table for each group
— one copy of *Dudley's Picnic* puzzle and table for each group
— one set of *PETS™ Tiles* shared between 2 or 3 groups
— a copy of *PETS™ Small Group Checklist* for each student

LESSON PLAN

1. Ask a parent or student volunteer to prepare a set of *PETS™ Tiles* before the lesson. Since color is one of the attributes of the *PETS™ Tiles*, teachers will need to make copies of each *PETS™ Tiles* blackline master on three different colors of paper or card stock. Teachers may want to laminate the sets for use year after year.

2. Group students into pairs or triads. The problems may also be done individually, but the "table conversation" among partners can be very enlightening to the teacher observing the group.

3. The task of each group is to use the clues and *PETS™ Tiles* to find the correct seating arrangement for the *PETS™* characters. The attributes of the tiles are size, shape, color and gender.

4. If time permits, have the group design its own table logic puzzle for other students to solve.

5. Answers may vary. Each solution must be checked against the clues for accuracy.

DIAGNOSTIC NOTES

Look for students who can quickly and accurately interpret the clues and arrive at a correct solution.

Some very able students will combine clues and ponder clues which do not give enough information at first but are useful later.

Other capable students may arrive at a correct answer without any intermediary steps, seeming to solve the puzzles intuitively. The design of their own table logic puzzles will provide insight into those students who are able to think deductively.

Look for students who devise subtle clues rather than obvious ones.

NOTES

PETS Tiles

Yolanda the Yarnspinner

Sybil the Scientist

Isabel the Inventor

Jordan the Judge

Max the Magician

Dudley the Detective

Sybil the Scientist

Yolanda theYarnspinner

Isabel the Inventor

Dudley the Detective

Jordan the Judge

Max the Magician

Sybil the Scientist

Max the Magician

Yolanda the Yarnspinner

Jordan the Judge

Dudley the Detective

Yolanda the Yarnspinner

Sybil the Scientist

Isabel the Inventor

Jordan the Judge

Max the Magician

Dudley the Detective

Jordan the Judge

Yolanda the Yarnspinner

Isabel the Inventor

Sybil the Scientist

Max the Magician

Dudley the Detective

Sybil the Scientist

Yolanda the Yarnspinner

Max the Magician

Dudley the Detective

Isabel the Inventor

Jordan the Judge

Isabel the Inventor

Yolanda's Literary Circle

2.

Author

1. All 6 animals came to the meeting of the Yolanda's Literary Circle.

2. Yolanda sits in the Author's Chair.

3. Yolanda is different in 1 way from the animals on either side of her.

4. Yolanda is different in 3 ways from the animal directly across from her.

5. Yolanda is different in 2 ways from the other animals at the table.

Fold or cut --

1.

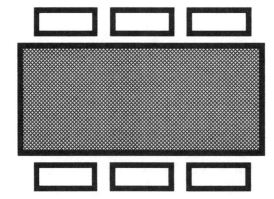

Dinner at Max's

1. All 6 animals are at the table.

2. All boys sit next to girls.
   All girls sit next to boys.

3. Each animal is different in 4 ways from the one sitting across from it.

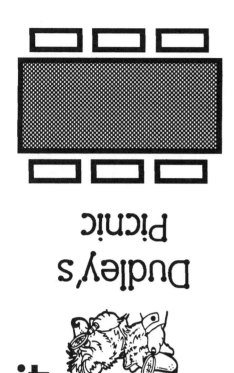

4. Dudley's Picnic

1. All 6 animals came to the picnic.

2. The 3 boys sat in a row on one side. The 3 girls sat across from them.

3. Each boy is different in 3 ways from the girl across from him.

4. Each boy and each girl is different in 1 way from his or her "elbow" neighbor.

Fold or cut --

3.

Jordan's Luncheon Party

1. All 6 animals are seated at the table.

2. Each boy will sit across from a girl.

3. No like colors will sit next to each other.

4. Each animal is different in 3 ways from the ones seated next to it.

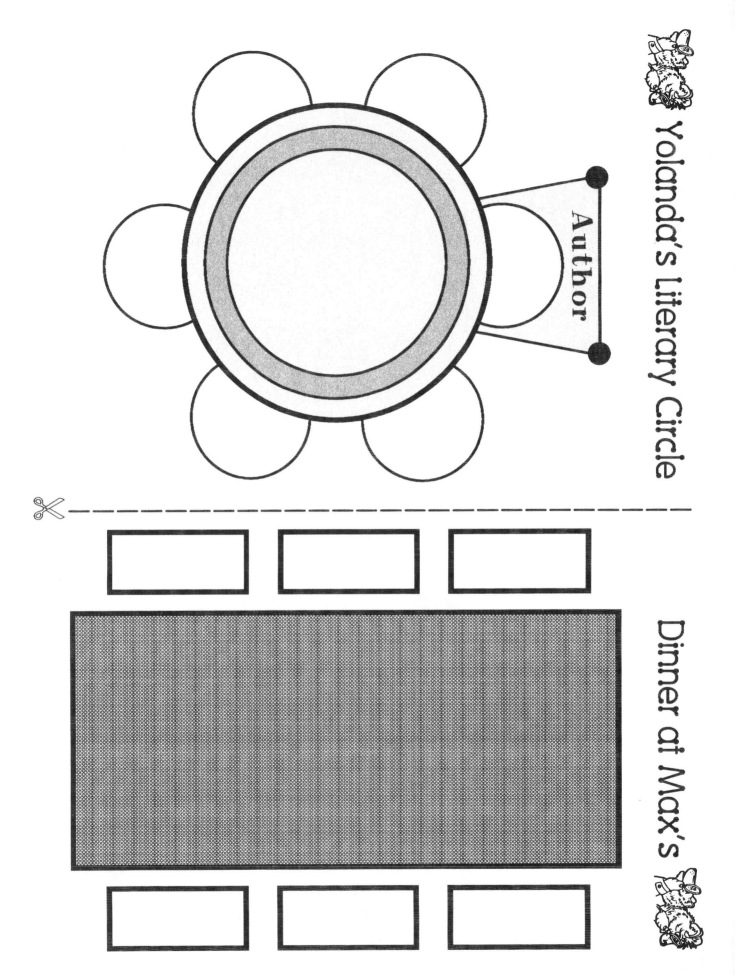

Author

Dinner at Max's

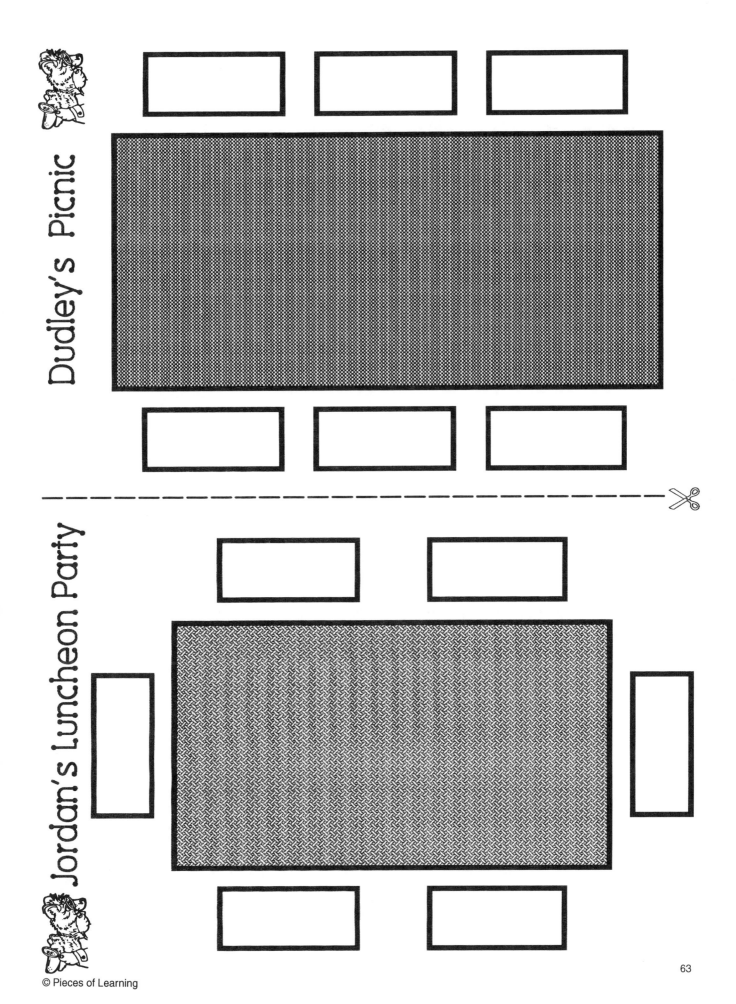

Dudley's Picnic

Jordan's Luncheon Party

63

PETS

List names of students as each behavior appears.
   Add checkmarks after name if behavior is repeated.
   Use a different color of ink or pencil for each whole group lesson.
	Behavioral Checklist
	---------- 	
	Divergent Thinking
	(Inventive/Creative)
		Teacher _____
		Grade: 1 __ 2 __ 3 __
		
		Date of whole 1. ____
		group instruction 2. ____
		               3. ____

OFFERS MANY IDEAS (fluency)	**OFFERS OFF-BEAT** AND/OR **ORIGINAL IDEAS** (originality)
ELABORATES ON AN IDEA BY ADDING DETAIL (elaboration)	**CHANGES COURSE** - STARTS NEW CATEGORIES (flexibility)
DISPLAYS AN UNUSUAL OR MATURE **SENSE OF HUMOR**	USES **ADVANCED VOCABULARY**
PETS classwork indicates an outstanding ability to use this thinking skill.	The following student/s did not participate during the thinking skills lessons, but I see these behaviors during regular class time.

In this unit, students are presented with the concepts of divergent thinking. Divergent thinking is necessary in many professions and is a vital part of the problem-solving process so critical to the 21st century. Isabel the Inventor uses divergent thinking strategies as she brainstorms and invents. Yolanda the Yarnspinner uses divergent thinking strategies as she creates colorful stories. Within a story setting, each will explain how she applies her thinking strategy and then the two divergent thinkers will partner to share their skills on a third activity.

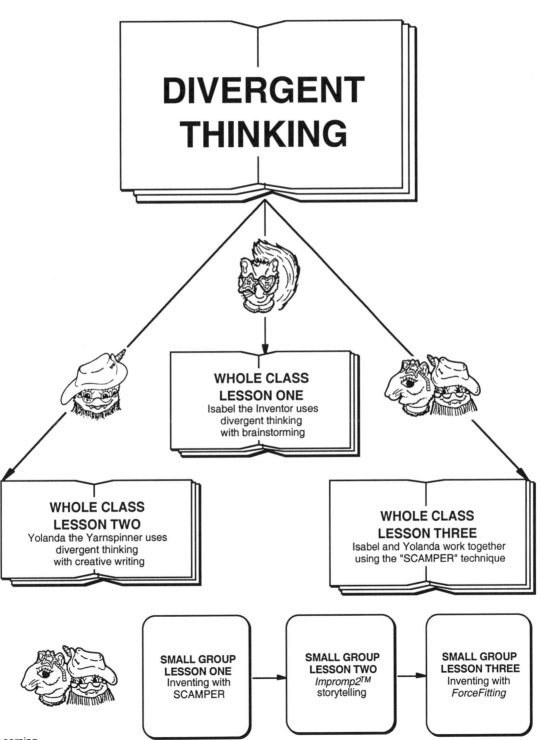

DIVERGENT THINKING

WHOLE CLASS LESSON ONE
Isabel the Inventor uses divergent thinking with brainstorming

WHOLE CLASS LESSON TWO
Yolanda the Yarnspinner uses divergent thinking with creative writing

WHOLE CLASS LESSON THREE
Isabel and Yolanda work together using the "SCAMPER" technique

SMALL GROUP LESSON ONE
Inventing with SCAMPER

SMALL GROUP LESSON TWO
Impromp2™ storytelling

SMALL GROUP LESSON THREE
Inventing with ForceFitting

DIVERGENT THINKING
WHOLE CLASS
LESSON 1

PURPOSE

The purpose of this lesson is to reinforce the inventive side of divergent thinking which includes brainstorming and seeing ordinary objects in new and unusual ways.

MATERIALS

— a copy of the story *Cloud Spinners*
— a blank overhead transparency and markers OR chart paper and markers
— an overhead transparency of *Variable Viewpoints* with the pictures cut apart
— a duplicated class set of *Rotation Creations*
— a duplicated class set of *Think...Turn...And Think Again!*
— *PETS™ Behavioral Checklist - Divergent Thinking*

LESSON PLAN

1. If students have completed **PRIMARY EDUCATION THINKING SKILLS I**, they learned about *inventive thinking.* As part of the PETS I lessons, students made Brainfocals™ which symbolized the ability to see ordinary objects in new and unusual ways. At this level, the term *divergent thinking* will be used instead of inventive thinking. The word **diverge** means to branch off in different directions, and that is what students will be encouraged to do as they think of many different ideas. If this is the first time students have been introduced to brainstorming, the following points need to be made:

— In divergent thinking there can be many correct responses.
— It is important to see things creatively.
— Ideas branch divergently from a common "stem."
— Piggybacking on the ideas of others is encouraged.

2. Read the story *Cloud Spinners* aloud to students, followed by *Variable Viewpoints.* Cut apart the shapes from *Variable Viewpoints* prior to the lesson. When doing this activity, it is not necessary to go through all the shapes; just brainstorm until the time is up. It is common for brainstorming to reach a lull. As this happens, turn the shape 90 degrees and continue brainstorming. Many times the most creative ideas will come after the lull.

CHALLENGE PAGES

Rotation Creations
Think...Turn...And Think Again!

3. Distribute *Rotation Creations*. Have students look at the rotated pictures and creatively add details to make the pictures into something unique and original. Have students use pencils rather than crayons to focus on a more detailed approach.

4. Distribute *Think...Turn...And Think Again*! Students choose one of the shapes at the bottom of the page, glue it in the center, rotate the page and brainstorm all the things that shape could be as the page is rotated.

DIAGNOSTIC NOTES

The following is a short summary of what to look for in the student behaviors and responses for Divergent Thinking, Whole Class 1:

OFFERS MANY IDEAS - All responses are acceptable. Look for students who provide many ideas. This reflects a student's fluency of thought. These responses do not have to be creative.

ELABORATES - This behavior would be displayed by a student who spends a long time adding details that may not occur to other students. Note students who piggyback on other students' ideas.

SENSE OF HUMOR - Many talented learners have an advanced sense of humor. These divergent thinking activities provide opportunities for students to display this sense of humor.

OFF-BEAT, ORIGINAL IDEAS - Look for students with ideas that are very different. These are responses that may not occur to other students. They are the responses that "stop you in your tracks."

ABILITY TO CHANGE COURSE - This reflects a student's flexibility of thought. Note students who are able to start new categories or responses. For example, if the class is brainstorming "green things" and many vegetables have been mentioned, the flexible thinker is the one who starts a new category, such as dollar bills. The *Think...Turn... Think Again!* activity further spotlights flexible thinking as students are asked to change their perceptions of a drawing each time they rotate the page.

ADVANCED VOCABULARY - Note the students who correctly use words other students their age may not know. They sound very adult in the way they express themselves.

Rotation Creations

Many creative solutions are possible for each of the pictures in *Rotation Creations.* Look for students whose ideas are unique. Give the original thinker credit for an off-beat idea.

Note students for flexible thinking if many categories are depicted in their drawings; for example, not all vases or all hats.

Note students whose overall drawings show a lot of detail.

Think...Turn...Think Again!

Look for students who "see" the unusual in the shape they choose to rotate.

Look for ideas that are beyond the obvious.

Look for a wide variety of categories to be represented on the idea list. The number of ideas is important but secondary to the uniqueness of ideas and number of categories.

NOTES

CLOUD SPINNERS

It was a beautiful autumn day and Isabel the Inventor was out collecting nuts to prepare for the long winter ahead. The orange and red leaves were gently falling to the ground, and the sky was a clear blue with big billowy clouds floating across it. As Isabel the Inventor continued looking for nuts, she noticed her friend Yolanda the Yarnspinner staring up through the treetops to the sky above. "Hi, Yolanda," said Isabel. "Are you taking a nap?"

"No, Isabel," replied Yolanda. "I just love to watch the clouds and the leaves as they fall and try to think of really wonderful words to describe what I see."

Isabel joined her friend on the ground. "I love to look at ordinary things such as clouds and see something unusual in them. Sometimes I use my *Brainfocals*™. They are glasses which help me focus my brain to think of unique ideas the way your bifocals focus your eyes."

"Unique!" exclaimed Yolanda. "That's a wonderful word. It means highly unusual or one of a kind."

"I don't have my *Brainfocals*™ with me, but I'm sure that together we can think of some very unique ideas. Let's make a list of all the unusual things we can see in the clouds," suggested Isabel.

"Isn't there a special word to use when a person thinks of many different ideas?" asked Yolanda.

"Yes, it is called **brainstorming**," answered Isabel.

"**Brainstorming!**" exclaimed Yolanda. "That's another great word. I love the ways I can picture that word in my head." *(Ask students how they picture the word **brainstorming**.)*

"Exactly how do you brainstorm?" wondered Yolanda.

"Well," explained Isabel, "**brainstorming** is a type of **divergent thinking**. Divergent comes from the word 'diverge' which means to go off in different directions. When I brainstorm, I try to think of many different ideas related to a main stem but branching off in different directions."

"Wow, that is really fascinating. It almost sounds as if you were describing that tree," noticed Yolanda.

"Yolanda, you are a great divergent thinker and using a tree to describe brainstorming is a wonderful idea. The trunk is like the stem or main idea. *(Put two fists on top of each other to symbolically show the stem.)* Let's brainstorm all of the things we can think of that are **round** or **go around**. That would be the stem."

"Let's see, balls are round and lollipops are round," Yolanda said.

"Yes, and now you are doing the branching part of brainstorming. *(Spread fingers to symbolically show branching.)* Balls and lollipops are different branches. When you said balls, it made me think of a basketball hoop. I branched from your branch. I am **piggybacking** when I do that," Isabel said excitedly.

"And lollipops made me think of an open mouth which is also round," added Yolanda. "I piggybacked off of my own idea. I'm going to write down our brainstorming ideas."

(At this point, give the students an opportunity to add to the list of things that are round or go around. The concept of "go around" is more abstract than an object that is round. Students who offer "clock hands go around" or "a cold goes around" show flexible thinking.)

"I love brainstorming," sighed Yolanda, "but I'm tired of thinking of all of the things that are round. Can we brainstorm something else?"

"Sure," said Isabel. "See that cloud up there?" *(Put the first picture from **Variable Viewpoints** on the overhead.)* Let's brainstorm all of the things we think the shape of that cloud could be."

"Isabel, we are so lucky to be divergent thinkers. Thinking of many ideas and seeing things in new and different ways is exciting!" exclaimed Yolanda the Yarnspinner as she happily continued writing down the flow of ideas she and her friend Isabel the Inventor were creating.

*(Give students an opportunity to brainstorm the first shape from **Variable Viewpoints**. Continue with the other shapes by asking students, "What do you think this might be?" Record student responses as they brainstorm ideas. When the brainstorming begins to lag or students begin to repeat responses, rotate the shape 90 degrees. This can be continued as long as desired.)*

Variable Viewpoints

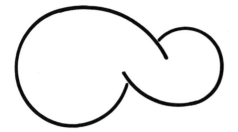

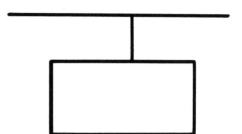

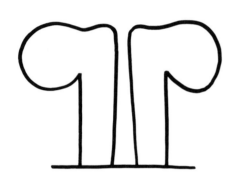

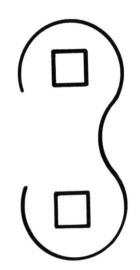

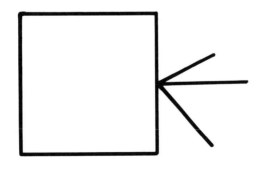

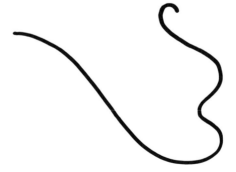

Name _____

Rotation Creations

What do you see? Use your imagination! Add details!

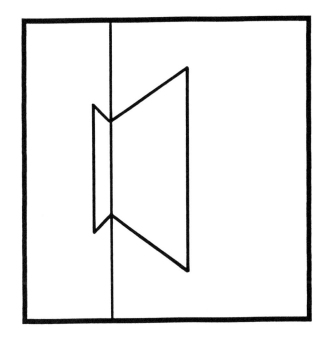

1. _____

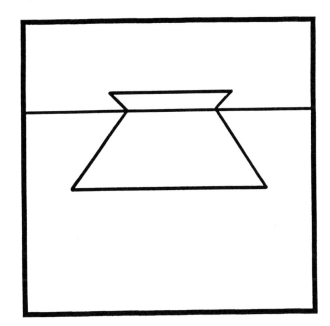

2. _____

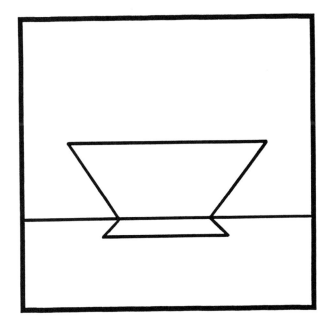

3. _____

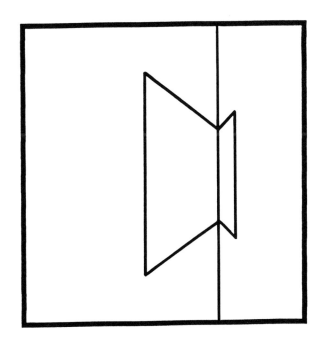

4. _____

Name_____

Think ... Turn ... And Think Again!

Cut out one shape from those at the bottom of the page. Glue it in the Idea Box in the middle of the page. Spin your page and think of all the things your shape could be!

1
2
3
4
5

5
4
3
2
1

1 _____
2 _____
3 _____
4 _____
5 _____

1
2
3
4
5

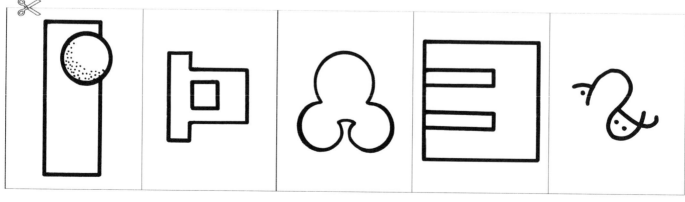

74

DIVERGENT THINKING
WHOLE CLASS
LESSON 2

PURPOSE

The purpose of this lesson is to practice divergent thinking skills as young writers are encouraged to brainstorm and use words creatively to add richness to their writing.

MATERIALS

— a copy of the story *Yolanda's Word Pictures*
— blank overhead transparencies and overhead transparency markers
— a duplicated class set of *The Creative Writer*
— *PETS™ Behavioral Checklist - Divergent Thinking*

LESSON PLAN

1. Review the characteristics of divergent thinking reinforced with Isabel the Inventor in Lesson 1. The characteristics include the following:

— There can be many correct responses.
— It is important to see things creatively.
— Ideas branch divergently from a common "stem."
— Piggybacking on the ideas of others is encouraged.

2. Yolanda the Yarnspinner, like Isabel the Inventor, sees many possibilities that begin from a common "stem." A creative imagination is very important for a storyteller. Ask students the ways in which Isabel the Inventor and Yolanda the Yarnspinner think alike. Possible responses include: Isabel and Yolanda both think of many ideas. They both create something that is original and unique. Isabel invents an object. Yolanda creates a story. They both put something together from parts and pieces, only Yolanda's pieces are words.

3. Read the story *Yolanda's Word Pictures* aloud to students. The main point of the story is to provide an opportunity to brainstorm colorful words, metaphors (a word picture created by the comparison of two unlikely words to convey a totally different meaning), alliteration (repetition of the same consonant sounds at the beginnings of words or in stressed syllables) and onomatopoeia (words that imitate sound). Use blank transparencies to record student responses. Keep the transparencies as a class word bank for original stories.

4. Have students use their unique words to write a story about a fall afternoon. Remind students to use colorful words and phrases to paint pictures that add richness to their stories. *The Creative Writer* is a blank page for story writing. In order to foster student creativity and elaboration, encourage students to use as many pages as they need or provide some other outlet for student stories.

5. No Challenge Page is included with this lesson. *The Creative Writer* may be started in class and finished in place of a Challenge Page.

6. This lesson might be made more real for students by taking a quiet field trip to a field or meadow. You can continue brainstorming in the meadow as students carefully listen and really look at their surroundings. Have students record in a journal words and thoughts or drawings to use later in their own story.

DIAGNOSTIC NOTES

The following is a short summary of what to look for in the student behaviors and responses for Divergent Thinking, Whole Class 2:

OFFERS MANY IDEAS - All responses are acceptable. Look for students who provide many ideas. These responses do not have to be creative.

ELABORATES - Look for students who enrich their stories with details or use phrases rather than single words to create a visual image or feeling. Also look for students who use metaphors, alliteration and onomatopoeia.

SENSE OF HUMOR - Many talented learners have an advanced sense of humor. These divergent thinking activities provide opportunities for students to display this sense of humor.

OFF-BEAT, ORIGINAL IDEAS - Look for students who offer words or phrases not thought of by anyone else. These are the "offbeat" responses that "stop you in your tracks."

ABILITY TO CHANGE COURSE - This reflects a student's flexibility of thought. Note students who are able to start new categories during brainstorming. Another example of student flexibility is the student who writes a story from the viewpoint of a spider or other meadow creature.

ADVANCED VOCABULARY - Look for students who understand the meanings of words beyond their grade level and use them correctly in their stories.

YOLANDA'S WORD PICTURES

Isabel the Inventor, who had recently taught her friend Yolanda the Yarnspinner how to brainstorm, was ready to do more brainstorming. She set off to find her friend in Crystal Pond Woods. After a short search, Isabel found Yolanda sitting at the edge of the meadow near the woods. "Yolanda," cried Isabel, "I've been looking for you! Do you want to do some more brainstorming?"

Yolanda quickly agreed. There was nothing Yolanda liked better than to sit cross-legged in her web thinking of wonderful words and unique ways to use them. "You know how much I love colorful words, so let's brainstorm words today."

Isabel frowned. "For you, words are easy," said Isabel. "I can think of inventions, but I have trouble thinking of exciting words to describe my inventions. How do you find the right words and put them together in just the right way?"

"Isabel, you are an inventor," explained Yolanda. "The pieces and how you put them together are like the words I use for my tales. First, I think about the story I want to tell. I envision the way I want my audience to feel. Then I choose exceptional words and weave them together to create a story."

"I think I'm beginning to understand," said Isabel, "but my stories could never be as interesting as the yarns you spin."

"Of course they can," answered Yolanda. "I'll show you. Let's brainstorm words together."

"What kind of words?" Isabel asked.

"M-m-m-m, let me think," answered Yolanda. "Let's brainstorm words about a meadow and a beautiful fall afternoon. We'll use special words that will make our readers feel the warmth of the sun, hear the sounds on the breeze, and in their 'mind's eye' see all the animals and insects of the meadow. We need words that are as colorful as flowers, such as **redwing, painted turtle,** and **green leaf hoppers**. We need action words such as **flutter, glide,** and **leap frogging**. We need lots of similes and metaphors which are words that create pictures, such as **wings spread like kites, dandelion fluff, raindrop jewels, maple wings, mushroom tables, firefly lights,** and a **cocoon snug in its sleeping bag**."

Isabel was catching on. She was very excited. Words just came tumbling out. "**Sunbeams, buzzing, mulberry tree, ribbit, clover, lily pad, rustling**."

"We need some characters," suggested Yolanda. "How about a **hop toad**, an **opossum**, some **ladybugs**, a **vole**, a **meadowlark**, or a **polliwog**?"

(Have students continue brainstorming colorful words to describe the animals and insects of the meadow. As prompts, ask students: What do they look like? How do they move? What are their sounds? Describe their homes. What do they remind you of? Encourage students to think creatively and stretch.)

Finally Isabel was exhausted. She and Yolanda had brainstormed a long list of very colorful and creative words. "Now is my favorite part!" exclaimed Yolanda the Yarnspinner, full of energy. "I am going to use some of these wonderful words and expressions to write a story about this beautiful fall afternoon in the meadow."

With that, she began to spin her autumn tale.

Author ______________________________

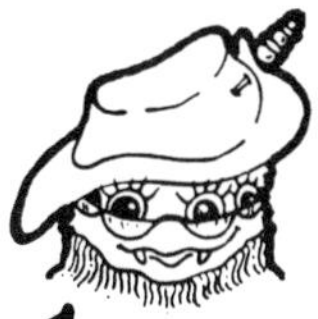

Title:

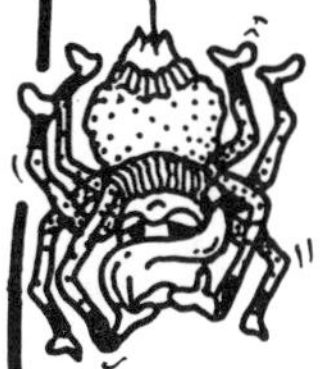

DIVERGENT THINKING
WHOLE CLASS
LESSON 3

PURPOSE

The purpose of this lesson is to review divergent thinking and introduce students to the SCAMPER* process.

MATERIALS

— one copy of the story *The Marvelous High Flying Kite*
— overhead transparency of *SCAMPER*
— a duplicated class set of *SCAMPERations!*
— a duplicated class set of *Crystal Clarion*
— *PETS™ Behavioral Checklist - Divergent Thinking*

LESSON PLAN

1. Review with students the divergent thinking skills presented by Isabel the Inventor who looks at things in unusual ways to generate many ideas and Yolanda the Yarnspinner who uses words to paint pictures and convey feelings.

2. Read the story *The Marvelous High Flying Kite* aloud to students. The main point of the story is to introduce students to the SCAMPER* process which is detailed below:

Substitute something
Combine things
Add something
Make parts smaller or bigger
Put the item or parts to another use
Eliminate something
Rearrange parts

3. Practice the SCAMPER process several times with students. Items that might be found at a yard sale, such as roller skates or hammocks, can provide a starting point.

4. The SCAMPER process can be difficult for students. Do not expect all students to master the process. As long as students are thinking divergently, then the lesson is successful.

* developed by Bob Eberle

CHALLENGE PAGES

SCAMPERations!
Crystal Clarion

5. It may be helpful to students if *SCAMPERations!* and *Crystal Clarion* are duplicated back to back. *SCAMPERations!* provides them with an opportunity to use the SCAMPER process. Instruct students to circle only one item to SCAMPER. In the left column, have students place a check mark in front of each line they use. In the SCAMPER column, ask students to write a phrase telling what they substituted, combined, added, etc. In the right hand column, ask students to draw their *SCAMPERation.*

6. When students write the *Crystal Clarion* news article about their *SCAMPERation*, the teacher may want to provide a list of "forbidden words" to force students to extend their written vocabulary and creative writing. Possible "forbidden words" are *thing*, *big*, and *great*.

DIAGNOSTIC NOTES

The following is a short summary of what to look for in the student behaviors and responses for Divergent Thinking, Whole Class 3:

OFFERS MANY IDEAS - All responses are acceptable. Look for students who provide many ideas. These responses do not have to be creative.

ELABORATES - Look for students who spend a long time adding details not thought of by other students. Note students who elaborate in the writing portion of the lesson.

SENSE OF HUMOR - Many talented students have an advanced sense of humor. Look for students whose writing shows a subtle or advanced sense of humor.

OFF-BEAT, ORIGINAL IDEAS - Look for students whose inventions are very different and unique. Look for students who use words or phrases not thought of by other students. These are the "off beat" ideas and responses that "stop you in your tracks."

ABILITY TO CHANGE COURSE - Note students who show, by idea and word choice, that they can consider a concept in more than one way. This is an example of flexibility.

ADVANCED VOCABULARY - Look for students who understand the meanings of words beyond their grade level and use them correctly in their writing.

SCAMPERation! and ***Crystal Clarion*** provide additional opportunities to look for the above characteristics. Encourage students to work independently so teachers can better assess divergent thinking characteristics.

THE MARVELOUS HIGH FLYING KITE

Springtime meant spring cleaning in Crystal Pond Woods, and that was a busy time for everyone. Sybil the Scientist was hard at work cleaning animal cages and going through the scientific journals she'd been writing over the long winter. Yolanda the Yarnspinner was busy dusting her web and sorting words for the new stories she would soon spin for the **Crystal Clarion**. Up in the hollow of the tallest oak tree in Crystal Pond Woods, Isabel was busy taking an inventory of the parts and ideas she would use for this year's inventions. Dudley the Detective was cleaning his attic and finding many wonderful and interesting clues. Sorting took him a while, for many of these were clues from the mysteries he had solved. He had to know just which clues to throw out and which to ponder for another mystery. Max the Magician had odds and ends of magic tricks, shapes, and patterns. Some of these would disappear with the spring cleaning.

There was, however, one creature in Crystal Pond Woods who was bothered by all the sorting and cleaning. This was Jordan the Judge. Being a practical owl, it bothered him to think of throwing out all this perfectly good stuff. "What's the best thing to do with all this paraphernalia?" he wondered. *(Brainstorm with students possible solutions for getting rid of the stuff. Possibilities may include calling a garbage truck or digging a deep hole next to the pond to bury it. Be sure to include having a garage sale.)*

After considering all of the possibilities, Jordan the Judge decided that having a neighborhood sale was the best idea. Not only was it ecologically safe, but so many things could also be reused in new and different ways. The residents of Crystal Pond Woods agreed and decided to hold the first annual Crystal Pond Woods Yard Sale.

Isabel the Inventor was thrilled. She could hardly wait to get her paws on her neighbors' fabulous stuff. It was not just junk. It was the stuff of which her dreams were made! "I'll be able to invent something truly marvelous, wondrous, and unbelievable!" she excitedly told her friends.

As things began to accumulate for the yard sale, Isabel could hardly decide what to choose first. She noticed Max carrying an old, slightly broken kite to the yard sale pile.

"Oh, Max!" Isabel cried. "I would love to take your kite and SCAMPER it."

Max looked very puzzled. "SCAMPER it? I have never heard the word SCAMPER used that way. Just what do you mean?"

"SCAMPER is another way of inventing something," explained Isabel. "You don't actually scamper, but each letter in the word SCAMPER stands for a way that an object can be changed."

"Will you show me how you are going to SCAMPER this old kite?" asked Max.

(Put the **SCAMPER** *overhead transparency on the projector.)*

"Sure," replied Isabel. "**S** stands for **substitute** something. Instead of this ratty old cloth tail on the kite, I am going to use this slightly bent metal Slinky® for a tail." After attaching the Slinky® to the kite, Isabel continued. "**C** stands for **combine** things. I think I will combine my kite with the workings of this transistor radio," mused Isabel as she picked up the radio.

Max the Magician was truly amazed. He often manipulated shapes but never quite in this way.

"**A** stands for **add** something." Isabel looked around and thought. As her eyes roamed the growing pile of stuff, she spotted a can of metallic paint. "I know what to add," she said with excitement. "I am going to paint the paper on the kite with this metallic paint so its shiny look will reflect the sun."

Max the Magician watched in awe. After painting her kite, Isabel went on to the next step in the SCAMPER process.

"**M** stands for **make** parts **smaller** or **bigger**," continued Isabel. "This transistor radio is really too big for my kite, so I am going to see if I can make it a little smaller in size." Isabel patiently worked on minifying the transistor radio. When she was finished, she called Max the Magician back over to continue explaining the process.

"**P** stands for **put** the item or parts of it to another use. Instead of using the radio to listen to music, I am going to use the radio to power the kite," Isabel enthusiastically explained. "I am also going to eliminate the string so my kite can go far distances. That is what the **E** stands for, **eliminating** something. And before I actually can send my marvelous kite on its high flying adventure, I need to rearrange the sticks to balance the radio for better flight."

"Let me guess," interrupted Max. "The **R** stands for **rearrange** parts."

"Max, you are correct. I think my new kite is ready for flight!"

By now, a small group had formed to watch Isabel the Inventor launch her kite. Yolanda had been especially interested. She needed a story for the **Crystal Clarion**, the local newspaper. Isabel's marvelous high flying kite was going to be the front page story. Everyone watched the kite take off and soar over the trees. When the kite was finally out  of sight, Yolanda turned to ask Isabel a few questions but Isabel was already hard at work creating another marvelous SCAMPERation.

Substitute something

Combine things

Add something

Make parts bigger or smaller

Put to another use

Eliminate something

Rearrange parts

Name_____

SCAMPERations!

Circle just one of these treasures left over from Isabel the Inventor's spring cleaning.

Now SCAMPER it in as many ways as you can to create a new and useful

SCAMPERation!!

	Tell how your treasure changed here:	Show how your treasure changed here:
Put a ✓ by each of the ways you SCAMPERed your treasure.	**S**ubstitute something	
	Combine things	
	Add something	
	Make it bigger or smaller	
	Put it to another use	
	Eliminate something	
	Rearrange parts	

86

✻ Crystal Clarion ✻

Serving the Crystal Pond Woods area since 1997

Vol. 1, No. 1

4 Acorns

_____
Today's Date

_____

_____

Headline

■ Local inventor develops new and amazing
SCAMPERation!

BY _____
     Your name

_____

_____

_____

_____

It's new and unusual
This SCAMPERation will change our world!

_____

_____

_____

_____

_____

_____

_____

_____

_____

_____

_____

_____

DIVERGENT THINKING
SMALL GROUP
LESSON 1

PURPOSE

The purpose of the lesson is to review and reinforce brainstorming and SCAMPERing. Students will also practice using colorful words as they try to sell their innovations.

MATERIALS

— a duplicated copy of *Scamper This!*
— a metal spinner, a brass paper fastener, and a metal washer
— a large sheet of drawing paper for each student
— a copy of *PETS™ Small Group Checklist* for each student

LESSON PLAN

1. Review with students the following main points of divergent thinking:

— There can be many correct responses.
— It is important to see things creatively.
— Ideas branch divergently from a common "stem."
— Piggybacking on the ideas of others is encouraged.
— Inventors often employ the SCAMPER process to help generate ideas.

Use the *SCAMPER* overhead transparency from Divergent Thinking, Whole Class 3 to remind students of the meaning of the acronym.

2. Prepare *Scamper This!* before class. A blackline master is provided. This may be cut out, colored, mounted on tagboard, and laminated. Attach the metal spinner to the center of *Scamper This!* with the brass paper fastener. Add the metal washer between the tagboard and the spinner for easier spinning.

3. Students will spin *Scamper This!* to determine the item they will be improving. The SCAMPER process will be used to make the improvements. They may select any combination of the SCAMPER approaches to help with the innovation.

4. Have students draw the SCAMPERized innovation as a detailed diagram with each important part labeled. Encourage elaboration in the designs.

5. After completing their diagrams, have students write brief advertisements about their designs. Suggest the "new and improved" qualities of their innovations be highlighted. Remind students that they are trying to sell their innovations and they need a persuasive tone. The following is an example of an advertisement:

It's new! It's WOW!! The amazing Locker Plus is the best locker ever made! It has a fiberglass door so that your locker won't get those ugly scratches. Also, it has a magnetized strip on the side of the door. Now, all you have to do is give your locker door a gentle push and it opens! Push it again and it closes. No more struggles with that stubborn handle!

On the inside, it has adjustable shelves, dividers, and hooks to fit the biggest coats and bookbags. The shelves can hold even the heaviest items! Plus, the dividers will adjust height to fit the shelves, no matter where you move them. You get all this and more for the low, low price of $39.99 each. Buy yours today!

Created by Sarah Pierce and Adam McNerney
Husmann Elementary School
Crystal Lake, Illinois

DIAGNOSTIC NOTES

Teachers will have the opportunity to use the students' innovations and advertisements as sources of assessment information. Look for students who have many ideas (fluency) for the SCAMPERing.

Also note those students who are able to use a number of different SCAMPER categories (flexibility).

Take note of exceptional originality of thought.

Look for students whose designs and/or advertisements show a great amount of detail (elaboration).

An advanced sense of humor in designing the innovation or in the writing of the advertisement is a good indicator of talent in divergent thinking.

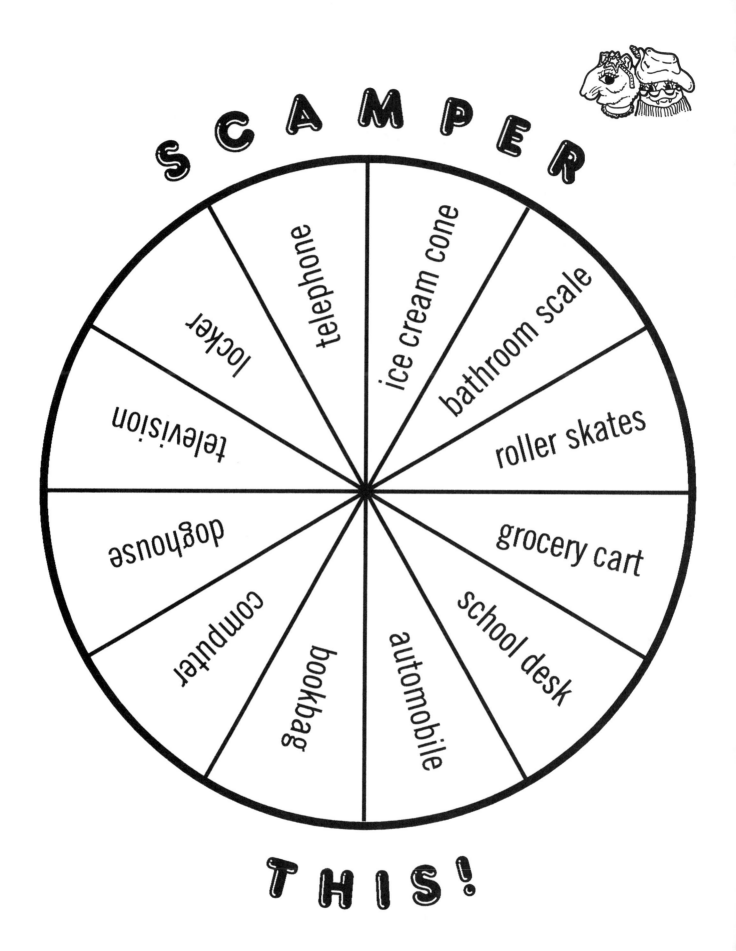

S C A M P E R

THIS!

telephone
ice cream cone
bathroom scale
roller skates
grocery cart
school desk
automobile
bookbag
computer
doghouse
television
locker

DIVERGENT THINKING
SMALL GROUP
LESSON 2

PURPOSE

The purpose of this lesson is to provide students with an opportunity to use words to develop a story creatively.

MATERIALS

— a deck of *Impromp2™ Cards*
— a duplicated set of *What If ...* story starters
— a copy of *PETS™ Small Group Checklist* for each student

LESSON PLAN

1. Review with students the following main points of divergent thinking:
   — There can be many correct responses.
   — It is important to see things creatively.
   — Ideas branch divergently from a common "stem."
   — Piggybacking on the ideas of others is encouraged.

2. *Impromp2™* is a creative game with words. The purpose of the game is for players to use the words on their cards to continue a story from the *What If ...* story starter. The teacher should be part of the group to model the process and redirect the story when necessary.

3. Deal each student and the teacher five *PETS™ Impromp2* cards. Using the words on the cards in plural form, -ing form, or modifying them is also acceptable. For example, a student who has the word *bowl* can use *bowls, bowling, shiny glass bowls,* or *heavy bowling ball* in the story. Model this before starting the story by using one of the dealt *Impromp2™* cards.

4. Begin by choosing and reading one of the *What If ...* story starters. The *What If ...* page may be folded and placed on the table for student reference. Have students take a few minutes to reflect on how their five words can become part of the story. Ask for a volunteer to begin the storytelling. If no one volunteers, the teacher may choose to start the story.

5. Proceed around the group giving each student a turn to continue the tale by using one of his or her words. A student may choose to pass. The story continues until everyone passes or all cards are used.

6. Encourage students to listen carefully to the sentences delivered by previous students. The flow of the story depends on whether students fit their sentences into the story in a way that makes sense. Additions to the story may include actions, descriptions, feelings, or other ideas that develop the story. The characters should be wiser or more mature by the end of the story.

DIAGNOSTIC NOTES

As students spin a story, look for students who are able to continue the story, building on previous items.

Note students who are adept with the vocabulary as well as students who elaborate with modifiers.

Seeing the whole picture, controlling the direction of the story, or introducing a problem for the characters to work through are far more difficult tasks than just adding one sentence after another. Look for students who are able to do this.

Note students who are able to add many elaborate details to the story.

Look for students whose flexible thinking allows them to continue the creative flow of the story without long pauses.

Another indication of talent in divergent thinking is a sophisticated sense of humor. Note students who naturally add this touch of humor.

NOTES

PETS Impromp2™ Cards

cave	pocket	stairs
pebble	cloud	trunk
wave	dust	sign
sock	lizard	band
treasure	monkey	puzzle
star	bowl	car
glasses	swing	magic

PETS Impromp2™ Cards

kaleidoscope	carrot	pony
balloon	bridge	skate
airplane	butterfly	frog
tunnel	mushroom	watch
snowball	zoo keeper	mouse
bumpy	growl	giggle
fly	bag	twitch

2. What If ...

Yesterday, quite by accident, we ended up right in the middle of Isabel the Inventor's newest chain-reaction contraption, "The Super Thing-A-Ma-Jig." I don't mind telling you that it took a whole lot of powerful thinking to escape to tell this tale ...

---

1. What If ...

One day while exploring in my attic, I found a funny-looking cabinet. The doors were stuck shut as though it hadn't been opened in many years. When I gave the handle a really hard yank ...

3. What If ...

You know what they say about uncorking a genie from a bottle. I never believed that could really be true until ...

---

4. What If ...

The other day in Crystal Pond Woods, Yolanda the Yarnspinner woke up to find more strange goings-on than she has legs! A mysterious package had suddenly appeared at Max the Magician's house ...

DIVERGENT THINKING
SMALL GROUP
LESSON 3

PURPOSE

The purpose of this lesson is to review and reinforce divergent thinking skills. The process of "force-fitting" will be used to enhance creativity, and students will design inventions related to their "forced-fit" words.

MATERIALS

- — one bag containing the *ForceFitting Nouns*
- — one bag containing the *ForceFitting Verbs*
- — a large sheet of drawing paper and markers or crayons for each student
- — a duplicated class set of *ForceFitting Spare Parts*
- — a copy of *PETS™ Small Group Checklist* for each student

LESSON PLAN

1. The teacher may want to copy *ForceFitting Nouns* on colored paper different from the color for *ForceFitting Verbs* to distinguish each group easily. One blank card is provided with each set should the teacher want to add additional words. Laminating the cards will allow use year after year.

2. Review with students the following main points of divergent thinking:

    - — There can be many correct responses.
    - — It is important to see things creatively.
    - — Ideas branch divergently from a common "stem."
    - — Piggybacking on the ideas of others is encouraged.

3. Give each student a sheet of drawing paper. Have students reach into each bag and draw out one *ForceFitting Noun* and one *ForceFitting Verb*.

4. Students are to "force-fit" their nouns and verbs to "invent" something new. For example, if the student draws the verb *stretch* and the noun *watermelon,* the two words must be used together to "invent" a new gizmo such as a *Watermelon Stretcher.*

5. The students are to diagram their inventions. They must use at least two of the items from *ForceFitting Spare Parts*; however, they may include more. Students may also draw in any additional parts their inventions need. It is important that students label the parts of their diagrams to facilitate evaluation. Have more capable students write about their inventions.

6. Teachers may want to have students actually build their inventions. This could be an extension project to the lesson.

DIAGNOSTIC NOTES

Look for students who have an abundance of ideas for their force-fit. This is an indication of fluent thinking.

Note those students who are able to change course and/or categories while designing their inventions. This indicates flexible thinking.

Students who come up with unique designs should be noted for their originality.

A great amount of detail is an indication of elaboration.

An advanced sense of humor displayed in the writing or the design of the invention is a good indicator of talent in divergent thinking.

NOTES

ForceFitting

Nouns

elephant		watermelon
refrigerator	bedroom slippers	rubber mouse
spaghetti	skyscraper	beetle
tornado	bathtub	pickle
peanut		bubble gum

	ForceFitting	
stretch	Verbs	lift
roll	wad	build
wash	bounce	stack
squeeze	smooth	wrap
chew		grow

ForceFitting  Spare Parts

P E T S

Behavioral Checklist

Visual Thinking

List names of students as each behavior appears.
    Add checkmarks after name if behavior is repeated.
    Use a different color of ink or pencil for each whole group lesson.

Teacher _____
Grade: 1 ___ 2 ___ 3 ___

Date of whole   1. _____
group instruction 2. _____
                3. _____

GRASPS CONCEPTS VERY QUICKLY	USES ONE CLUE TO DETERMINE ANOTHER OR PUTS CLUES TOGETHER - **SEES THE INTERRELATIONSHIP OF VISUAL CLUES**
COMMENTS OR BEHAVIORS INDICATE AN ABILITY TO **MANIPULATE/INTERPRET SHAPES MENTALLY**	DEMONSTRATES **FLEXIBILITY OF PERSPECTIVE** - TRIES A VARIETY OF APPROACHES
INTUITIVELY SEES ANSWERS WITHOUT INTERMEDIATE STEPS	**DISPLAYS LONG ATTENTION SPAN** - WORKS EXERCISE DILIGENTLY TO THE END
PETS classwork indicates an outstanding ability to use this thinking skill.	The following student/s did not participate during the thinking skills lessons, but I see these behaviors during regular class time.

In this unit, students are presented with the concepts of visual thinking. This type of thinking, often neglected in traditional school work, is necessary in a variety of daily activities and is a vital part of many occupations. In this type of thinking, students use their right brain hemispheres to manipulate shapes mentally. Within story settings, Max the Magician provides opportunities for honing visual thinking, first on his own, then with Yolanda the Yarnspinner, and finally with Dudley the Detective and Sybil the Scientist.

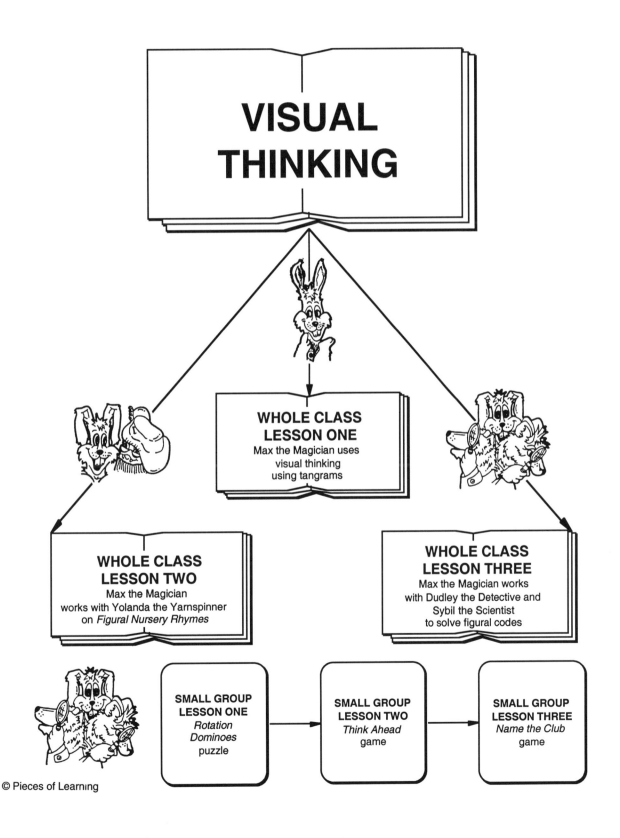

VISUAL THINKING

WHOLE CLASS LESSON ONE
Max the Magician uses visual thinking using tangrams

WHOLE CLASS LESSON TWO
Max the Magician works with Yolanda the Yarnspinner on *Figural Nursery Rhymes*

WHOLE CLASS LESSON THREE
Max the Magician works with Dudley the Detective and Sybil the Scientist to solve figural codes

SMALL GROUP LESSON ONE
Rotation Dominoes puzzle

SMALL GROUP LESSON TWO
Think Ahead game

SMALL GROUP LESSON THREE
Name the Club game

VISUAL THINKING
WHOLE CLASS
LESSON 1

PURPOSE

The purpose of this lesson is to reinforce the concepts of visual thinking through the mental manipulation of shapes. Students will be manipulating tangrams to replicate a given design.

MATERIALS

- a copy of the story *Max and His Shadowy Shapes*
- a set of solid tangrams; do NOT use the transparent ones designed for the overhead projector
- an overhead projector
- either a duplicated class set of *Max's Tangrams* or a commercial set of tangrams for each student
- folders to set around student desks to screen their work from the eyes of their neighbors (optional)
- a duplicated class set of *Leave One Out: Brianna Butterfly*
- a duplicated class set of *Leave One Out: Belinda Butterfly*
- a duplicated class set of *Leave One Out: Felix Fish*
- a duplicated class set of *Leave One Out: Tobias Turtle*
- *PETS™ Behavioral Checklist - Visual Thinking*

LESSON PLAN

1. Review with students the thinking skills learned thus far. The discussion should include the terms *convergent* and *divergent*. Help the students to re-define as well as contrast these thinking styles as part of the review process.

Max the Magician is a PETS™ character who uses his right brain hemisphere to manipulate mentally the shapes he sees. Characteristics of visual thinking are:

- Thinking skills do not occur in isolation; visual thinking combines analysis of visual clues, logical deduction, flexibility of perspective, and fluency of thought.
- The eyes and brain must work together to think about given information.
- Tolerance of ambiguity and perseverance are important components.

2. Distribute *Max's Tangrams* or a commercial set of 7 tangrams to students. Review the names of the tangram pieces (small, medium, and large triangles [5], a square, and

a parallelogram). To ensure individual solutions, the teacher may wish to have students set up folders at their desks for privacy.

3. Read the story of *Max and his Shadowy Shapes* aloud. During the story, ask students to replicate a shadow shape shown on the overhead projector using the tangram pieces at their desks. Explain that their solutions must match the tangrams on the overhead projector exactly. This is an important part of the assessment of the ability to see and manipulate the shapes.

4. The puzzles in the story progress from easier designs to more difficult, complex designs. When putting the puzzles on the overhead projector, carefully arrange the tangram pieces while the light is off. Push pieces together closely so that no light will shine through between the individual pieces. When the design is complete, turn on the overhead projector's light, creating a shadow of the completed design on the screen. Students should examine the shape and arrange their pieces to replicate the puzzle they see. An alternative to using actual tangrams to make the shadows on the overhead projector is to make paper copies of the puzzles, cut them out and place them on the overhead. Although this method is easier for the teacher, it does not allow the students to see that the original shadow was made by specifically placed tangram pieces.

5. Give students plenty of time to replicate the shapes. Then reveal the solution by separating the tangram pieces slightly on the overhead to allow a bit of light to shine around the individual pieces and show their borders. Using overhead transparencies of the story illustrations is another method for revealing the solutions. Be aware that some of the finished puzzles can be created in more than one way. Accept any response that correctly gives the final shape, as long as accurate proportions are maintained. Students who offer viable alternative solutions may be showing aptitude for visual thinking.

CHALLENGE PAGES

Leave One Out: Brianna Butterfly *Leave One Out: Belinda Butterfly*
Leave One Out: Felix Fish *Leave One Out: Tobias Turtle*

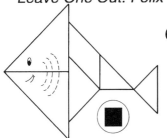

6. Distribute the Challenge Pages to students. *Leave One Out* requires students to cover a shape using six of the tangram pieces. Ask students to outline the tangram pieces after covering the puzzle and then to circle the tangram piece that was not used.

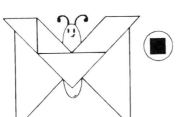

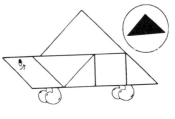

DIAGNOSTIC NOTES

The following is a short summary of what to look for in student behaviors and responses for Visual Thinking, Whole Class 1:

GRASPS CONCEPTS - Look for students who quickly see how to make the shapes presented. Note every time a student correctly completes a puzzle.

SEES INTERRELATIONSHIP OF CLUES - Look for students who will use all available clues. The comments made as the students work are excellent indicators of their thinking processes. Record students whose comments depict good spatial reasoning, such as "the two small triangles make the same shape as the parallelogram," or "that must be the medium triangle; the small triangle doesn't look right."

MANIPULATES/INTERPRETS SHAPES MENTALLY - Note any student who creates a correct answer without excessive physical manipulation of the tangram pieces.

FLEXIBILITY OF PERSPECTIVE - Look for students who think flexibly about the shapes and are willing to try many approaches.

INTUITIVELY SEES ANSWERS - Look for students who just seem to know where the tangram pieces go. They may consistently have the correct answers without knowing how they got those answers.

DISPLAYS LONG ATTENTION SPAN - Students who "don't get it" have a tendency to give up easily. Look for students who have a tolerance for ambiguity and who will persevere to reach a puzzle solution. Also look for students who derive a great amount of excitement from these activities.

Leave One Out

Important in the identification portion of this lesson will be those students who are able to complete these Challenge Pages correctly and independently. Note these students in the appropriate box at the bottom of the *PETS™ Behavioral Checklist - Visual Thinking.*

NOTES

MAX AND HIS SHADOWY SHAPES

Once a week in Crystal Pond Woods, all the forest creatures like to get together for a community campfire where they take turns singing songs, telling stories, and entertaining one another. This week, Max the Magician wanted to do something special because it was his turn to entertain his friends. He thought and thought about what he could do that would be really fun. He remembered how his grandfather had entertained Max and his brothers and sisters with shadow plays in front of the light. Max's favorite had always been when Grandfather made rabbit ears from his paws.

Suddenly, Max knew just what he would do. He dug into his chest of favorite things and pulled out a set of tangrams. Max loved all the shapes he could make with these seven geometric pieces. He would tell an exciting story using his tangram shapes. Max would be the hit of the evening.

That night, as all his friends gathered around the campfire, Max began his tale:

"The other day, I went out to my garage."

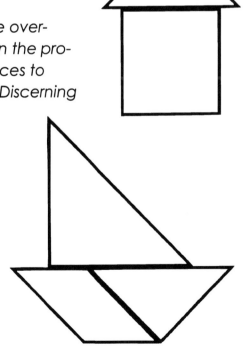

(Place the square and small triangle on the overhead projector to make the house shape. Turn on the projector. Ask students to use their own tangram pieces to replicate exactly what is showing on the screen. Discerning eyes will select the correct triangle to use. When most students have completed the "garage," show them the correct answer by pushing the pieces apart on the overhead. Turn off the projector. Then continue with the story.)

"I got out my sailboat to take to the lake."

(Create the shape and turn on the projector. Take time to monitor students for accurate responses.)

"It was a beautiful day, and as I walked to the lake, I met Ellen Eagle. She asked to come along with me, so off we went together."

(Create the shape.)

"When we got to the lake, there sat Sam the Siamese cat."

(Create the shape.)

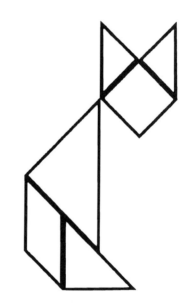

"We all sailed my boat on the lake and had lots of fun. Then, we decided to go play at home."

(Seven pieces are used to make the house shape. This is quite difficult for students to replicate and may take some time. Be sure to encourage complete accuracy.)

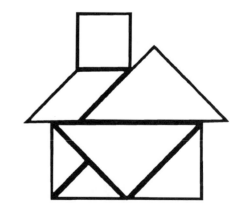

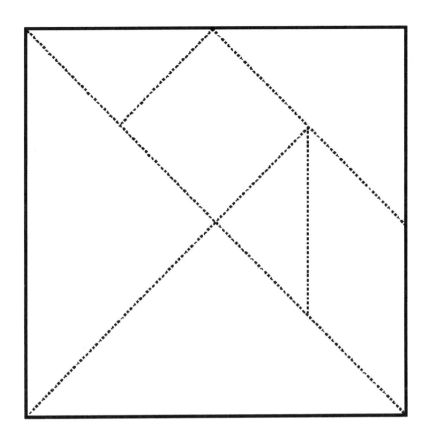

Max's
Tangrams

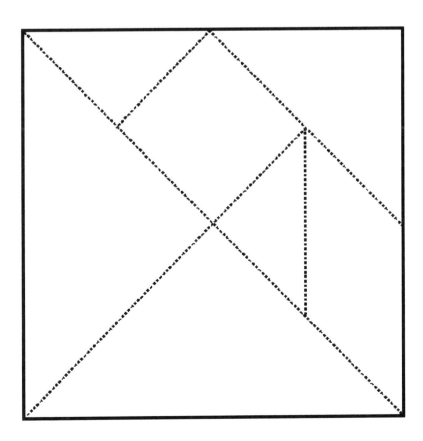

Max's
Tangrams

Leave One Out:
Brianna Butterfly

Use a set of Max's Tangrams to create wings for Brianna Butterfly.
Carefully trace around each piece in your solution.

Now circle the tangram piece you did NOT use:

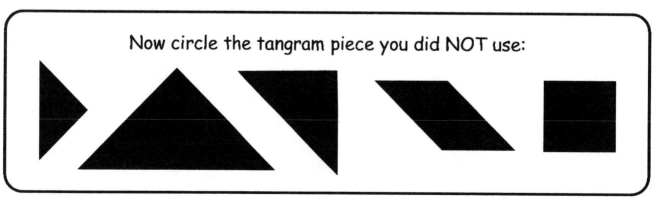

Name_____

Leave One Out: Belinda Butterfly

Use a set of Max's Tangrams to create this beautiful butterfly.
Carefully trace around each piece in your solution.

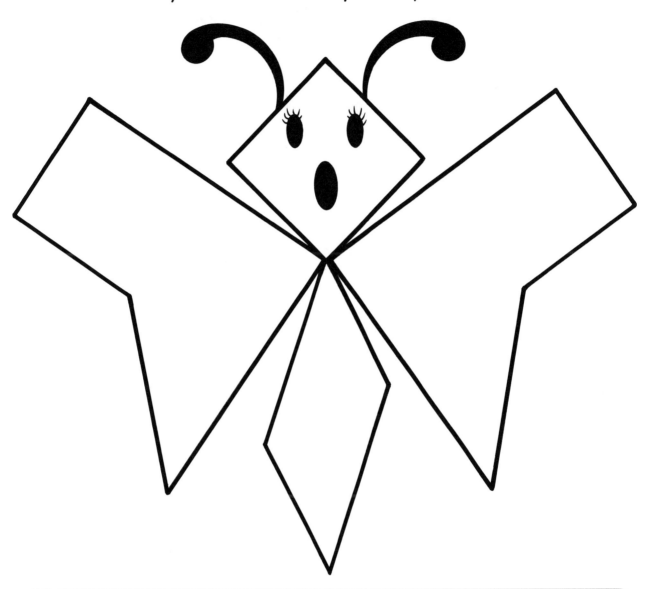

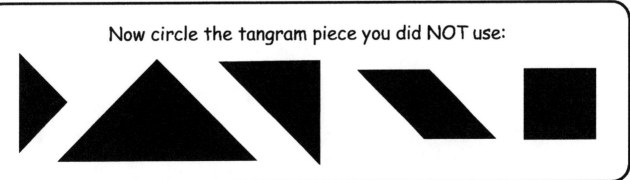

Now circle the tangram piece you did NOT use:

Name_____

Leave One Out: Felix Fish

Use a set of Max's Tangrams to create this fish that lives in Crystal Pond.
Carefully trace around each piece in your solution.

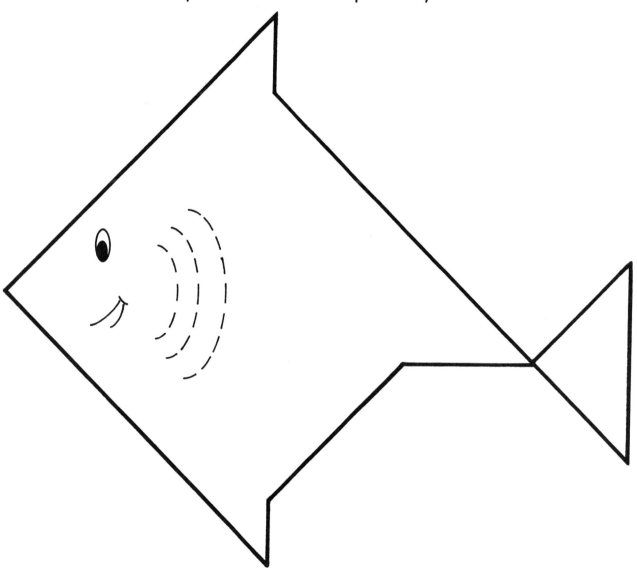

Now circle the tangram piece you did NOT use:

Name_____

Leave One Out:
Tobias Turtle

Use a set of Max's Tangrams to create this turtle from Crystal Pond Woods.
Carefully trace around each piece in your solution.

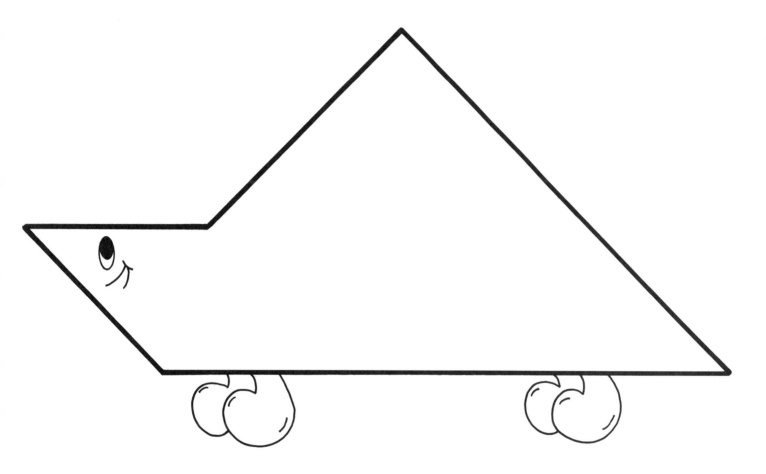

Now circle the tangram piece you did NOT use:

VISUAL THINKING
WHOLE CLASS
LESSON 2

PURPOSE

The purpose of this lesson is to combine visual thinking and storytelling to solve and then to create nursery rhymes with abstract shapes instead of words.

MATERIALS

— a copy of the story *Nursery Rhymes in Disguise*
— an overhead transparency of *Once upon a time...1*
— an overhead transparency of *Once upon a time...2*
— an overhead transparency of *Once upon a time...3*
— a duplicated class set of *Once upon a time...4*
— a duplicated class set of *Once upon a time...5*
— a duplicated class set of *Once upon a time...6*
— a duplicated class set of *Once upon a time...7*
— *PETS™ Behavioral Checklist - Visual Thinking*

LESSON PLAN

1. Review with students the special kind of thinking that Max the Magician does. Students need to think about the type of thinking they are doing. Characteristics of visual thinking are:

— Thinking skills do not occur in isolation; visual thinking combines analysis of visual clues, logical deduction, flexibility of perspective, and fluency of thought.
— The eyes and brain must work together to think about given information.
— Tolerance of ambiguity and perseverance are important components.

2. Read the story *Nursery Rhymes in Disguise* aloud to students. These are the main points of the story:

— Figures and shapes are used as clues to capture the story of a nursery rhyme.
— The size and placement of shapes and figures within the frame are clues to the nursery rhyme.
— Student responses should be tested frame by frame.

3. During the reading of the story, display the overhead transparency *Once upon a time...1*. Students are to identify this nursery rhyme. If students name fairy tale titles instead of nursery rhymes, discuss the difference between nursery rhymes and fairy tales. When a student correctly identifies the figural nursery rhyme as **Jack and Jill**, point out each frame of the nursery rhyme while the student recites it.

4. The figural nursery rhyme *Once upon a time...2* is the nursery rhyme **Little Miss Muffett**. Many students may guess **Hey Diddle Diddle** or **Twinkle, Twinkle Little Star** because of the star in the fourth panel. Should this happen, go back to *Once upon a time...1* and demonstrate that the shapes are abstract representations of the verse. The star in the second rhyme does not stand for a real star. This rhyme usually takes a bit longer to figure out. Give students clues by indicating the addition of shapes in each successive frame. The figural nursery rhyme *Once upon a time...3* is the nursery rhyme **Itsy Bitsy Spider**.

CHALLENGE PAGES

Once upon a time...4 (**Humpty Dumpty**)
Once upon a time...5 (**Hickory Dickory Dock**)
Once upon a time...6 (**Georgie Porgie**)
Once upon a time...7 (**Blank**)

5. Distribute the Challenge Pages. It may help to brainstorm as a class some nursery rhyme titles and recite the rhymes with the students. Remind students that each frame represents a line or part of a line of verse. *Once upon a time...7* is a set of blank frames for students to create their own figural nursery rhymes. The shapes they use should be abstract, not real representations of the items in the rhyme.

DIAGNOSTIC NOTES

The following is a short summary of what to look for in student behaviors and responses for Visual Thinking, Whole Class 2:

GRASPS CONCEPTS - Look for students who quickly and accurately grasp the concept of abstract figures representing the characters and events in nursery rhymes. These students will relish the abstractness of the figures.

SEES INTERRELATIONSHIP OF CLUES - Look for students who ponder the given clues rather than guessing the nursery rhymes randomly. In addition, look for students who create innovative and original figural rhymes by using shapes together in clever ways.

MANIPULATES/INTERPRETS SHAPES MENTALLY - Look for students who successfully manipulate the abstract shapes in such a way that the actions of the rhyme are readily apparent.

FLEXIBILITY OF PERSPECTIVE - Look for students who are able to view a shape in different and unique ways. These students are not bound to the literal interpretation of shapes. They can change their perspectives in order to fit abstract shapes to the characters of the rhymes.

INTUITIVELY SEES ANSWERS - Look for students who seem to understand the abstract nature of the activity intuitively. They may blurt out the correct answer immediately without having to study the puzzle frame by frame.

DISPLAYS LONG ATTENTION SPAN - Students who "don't get it" have a tendency to give up easily. Look for students who have a tolerance for ambiguity and perseverance for these type of puzzles.

Once upon a time...4 ,5, and *6* involve convergent and visual thinking. Note students who display strong convergent thinking skills as well as strong visual thinking skills. *Once upon a time...7* combines divergent and visual thinking. Note students who are able to apply what they have learned to create a figural nursery rhyme accurately. Look for the innovative use of shapes.

NOTES

NURSERY RHYMES IN DISGUISE

Yolanda the Yarnspinner is well known throughout Crystal Pond Woods for her wonderful stories. She uses very colorful words to make her stories come alive. But, like all the creatures in Crystal Pond Woods, Yolanda loves to be challenged by thinking puzzles. One day Yolanda decided to make a story with figures and shapes instead of words. Since Max the Magician is very good at visual thinking, Yolanda wanted Max to help her with this special kind of story.

"Max," asked Yolanda, "I want to try something new, and I need your help. I want to capture the story of a nursery rhyme by turning it into a picture of figures and shapes. I am going to call it a figural nursery rhyme."

Max thought this was a very creative idea. "Let's begin right away!" he exclaimed. "We can share our puzzles at next week's community campfire."

Yolanda, using a toadstool for a seat, began to spin for Max her vision of a nursery rhyme with figures and shapes. "Our perplexing puzzle has six frames. Each frame is a significant piece of the rhyme. In order to make the puzzle more challenging to solve, the shapes are not intended to resemble the things in the rhyme."

"I think I'm beginning to understand," said Max. "The toadstool you are sitting on could be a rectangle or a circle."

"Yes," responded Yolanda, warming to her topic. "And depending on its size and how it is positioned in the frame, a triangle could be a divine hat, a wee person, or an elegant shoe. Let me show you what I mean," she continued. "See if you can figure out this figural nursery rhyme."

*(Place the overhead transparency of **Once upon a time...1** on the overhead.)*

Max studied the frames looking for clues. "Let me think," he said, scratching his whiskers.

*(Give students an opportunity to identify the rhyme. Students should notice that certain shapes are repeated throughout the frames, while other shapes are added to further define the rhyme. If students incorrectly identify the rhyme, rather than simply saying "No," try the nursery rhyme to see if it works. Recite the rhyme line by line to see if it fits all the clues frame by frame. If too many clues are not satisfied, students should be able to see that the rhyme does not fit. The figural nursery rhyme **Once upon a time...1** represents the nursery rhyme **Jack and Jill.**)*

When Max correctly identified the nursery rhyme, Yolanda knew that he was catching on. "Would you like to compose a figural nursery rhyme, Max?" Yolanda asked.

"Yes!" cried Max. "I have a great idea! Wait while I draw my figural nursery rhyme for you to guess." Max quickly drew a number of shapes in the frames.

*(Place **Once upon a time...2** on the overhead projector.)*

"Ooh, Max, you are really marvelous at this! This is a deliciously difficult puzzle. Let me think about it," replied Yolanda as she bent her head in thought.

*(Give students an opportunity to identify the rhyme. Again, test student answers frame by frame. This figural nursery rhyme represents **Little Miss Muffett.**)*

"You are exceedingly talented at this, Max," complimented Yolanda. "Now I have another one for you to try."

*(Place **Once upon a time...3** on the overhead projector. Give students an opportunity to identify this rhyme. It represents **Itsy Bitsy Spider.**)*

 Max the Magician and Yolanda the Yarnspinner continued to create figural nursery rhymes for the creatures of Crystal Pond Woods to solve. This week's community campfire is going to be a very challenging experience!

This is a nursery rhyme.
Can you recite it by "reading" the pictures made with symbols?

∅ Once upon a time ...   1 &

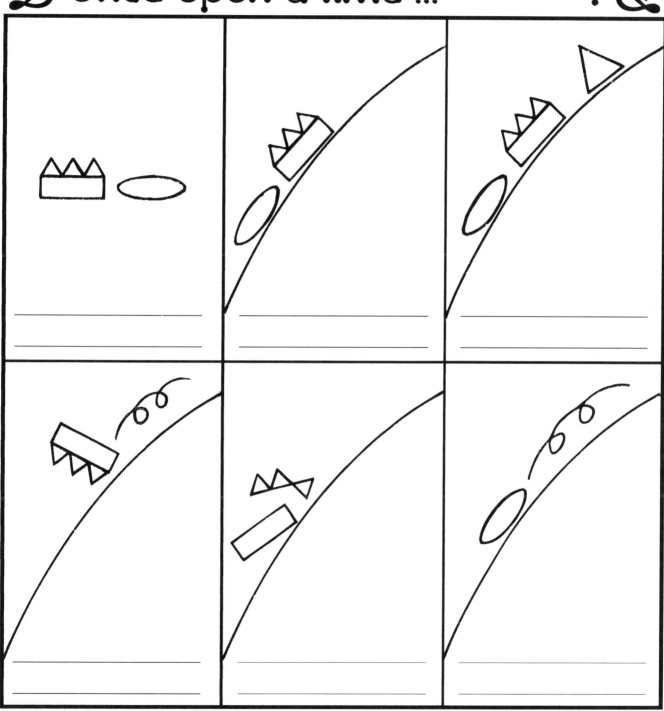

∅ The End &

This is a nursery rhyme.
Can you recite it by "reading" the pictures made with symbols?

℘ Once upon a time ...   2℘

℘ The End ℘

This is a nursery rhyme.
Can you recite it by "reading" the pictures made with symbols?

Name _____

This is a nursery rhyme.
Recite it to yourself by "reading" the pictures made with symbols.
Write down the words that go with the pictures in each of the boxes.

✆ Once upon a time ...   4 ✆

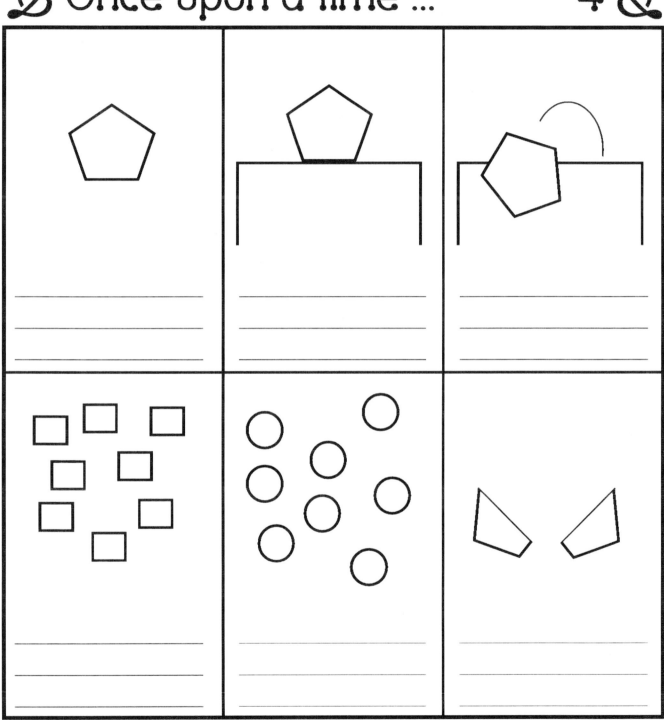

✆ The End ✆

Name _____

This is a nursery rhyme.
Recite it to yourself by "reading" the pictures made with symbols.
Write down the words that go with the pictures in each of the boxes.

℘ Once upon a time ...   5 ℛ

℘ The End ℛ

123

Name _____

This is a nursery rhyme.
Recite it to yourself by "reading" the pictures made with symbols.
Write down the words that go with the pictures in each of the boxes.

◌ Once upon a time ...   6 ◌

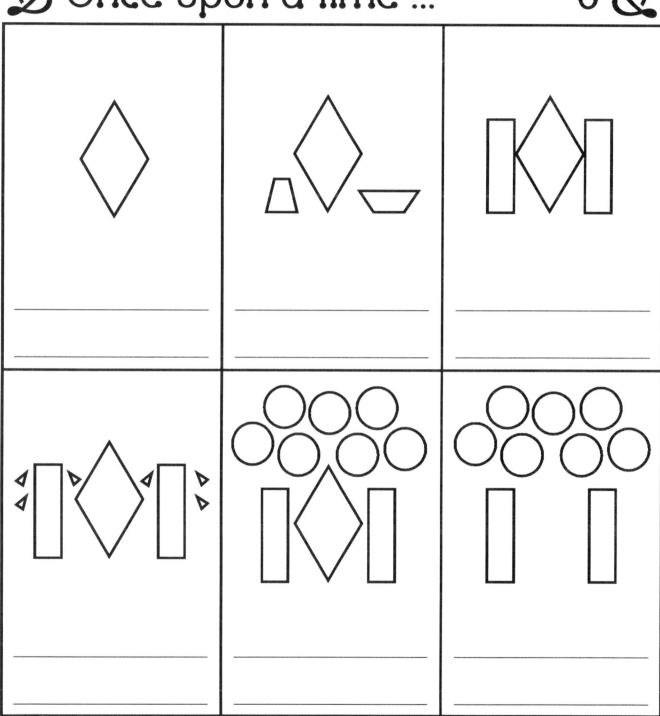

◌ The End ◌

Name _____

Choose a favorite nursery rhyme.
Use symbols instead of words to tell the story in these six boxes.
Write the rhyme on the back of this paper.

℘ Once upon a time ... 7 ℘

℘ The End ℘

VISUAL THINKING
WHOLE CLASS
LESSON 3

PURPOSE

The purpose of this lesson is to reinforce the concepts of critical thinking using visual and convergent thinking skills to decode messages.

MATERIALS

- — a copy of the story *The Puzzlers' Club*
- — an overhead transparency of *Max's Mystery Message*
- — a duplicated class set of *Sybil's Cipher*
- — a duplicated class set of *Hexagon Hieroglyphics*
- — a duplicated class set of *Creative Cryptography*
- — PETS™ Behavioral Checklist - Visual Thinking

LESSON PLAN

1. Review with students the characteristics of visual thinking emphasized in earlier lessons. Include in the discussion how visual thinking is related to convergent and divergent thinking. Characteristics of visual thinking are:

- — Thinking skills do not occur in isolation; visual thinking combines analysis of visual clues, logical deduction, flexibility of perspective, and fluency of thought.
- — The eyes and brain must work together to think about given information.
- — Tolerance of ambiguity and perseverance are important components.

2. Read the story *The Puzzlers' Club* aloud to students. The object of the story is to have students use what they have learned about visual and convergent thinking while working with codes.

3. In the story, some strategies for decoding are provided. Students may be able to decode *Max's Mystery Message* faster than it is decoded by the characters in the story. If so, have them verbalize their methods to use as strategies for future codes. Some strategies for solving codes are:

- — Letters that follow apostrophes are usually **S** or **T**.
- — Single letter words are usually **A** or **I**.
- — Write the same letter below all identical symbols.
- — Look for doubled symbols. Not all letters can be doubled.

— Nearly all two-letter words consist of a vowel and a consonant.
— The most common three-letter words are **THE** and **AND**.
— Some codes are not random and can be deciphered by
    determining the pattern.

4. Distribute *Sybil's Cipher* to students. *Sybil's Cipher* is a picture
code. To decode the message, students need to write the first letter
of each animal picture. After decoding the message, be sure to discuss with students
the pattern to this system. The message is: **The password to the club is cipher.**

5. Distribute *Hexagon Hieroglyphics* to students. *Hexagon Hieroglyphics* is a shape
code that is more challenging than the previous codes. There is a pattern to the designs
assigned to each letter of the alphabet, and using this pattern may help students
decode the message. Three of the letters have been supplied. Teachers may choose to
block out these letters prior to copying if a more challenging code is desired. The
message is: **Bring a great puzzle to the first club meeting at Sybil's lab.** The
correct key code is:

Hexagon Hieroglyphics

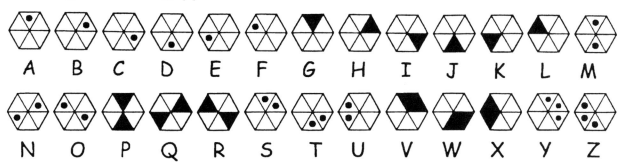

Some students find it easier to discern the code's pattern if they have 26 blank hexagons they can fill in as they determine different letters. Put these blank hexagons, each matched with a letter of the alphabet, on the back of *Hexagon Hieroglyphics*.

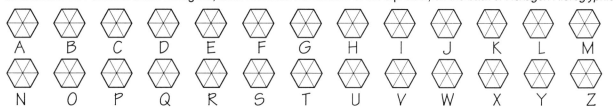

CHALLENGE PAGE

Creative Cryptography

6. *Creative Cryptography* is an opportunity for students to design an original code key.
Encourage students to develop a code with a pattern in the same way as *Sybil's Cipher*
and *Hexagon Hieroglyphics* followed a pattern. The goal of *Creative Cryptography* is to
create a code that can be decoded using logical reasoning rather than having to refer to
the code key. Coded messages should be written on a separate sheet of paper. These
can then be given as puzzles for other students to decode.

DIAGNOSTIC NOTES

The following is a short summary of what to look for in student behaviors and responses for Visual Thinking, Whole Class 3:

GRASPS CONCEPTS - Look for students who quickly decode and encode. These are students who are more able to differentiate symbols and associate them with the correct letter.

SEES INTERRELATIONSHIP OF CLUES - Look for students who will use all available clues or ideas to try and figure out the pattern. In addition, look for students who recognize they have made errors in either decoding or encoding and correct their mistakes.

MANIPULATES/INTERPRETS SHAPES MENTALLY - There are many ways to solve codes. Look for students who forego the strategies and easily associate shapes with letters.

FLEXIBILITY OF PERSPECTIVE - Look for students who think flexibly about the shapes and are willing to try many approaches.

INTUITIVELY SEES ANSWERS - Look for students who seem to understand intuitively the codes presented. They may have the correct answer without being able to explain their methods.

DISPLAYS LONG ATTENTION SPAN - Some students will especially enjoy this activity. An enthusiasm towards codes may indicate talent in this area.

Sybil's Cipher and Hexagon Hieroglyphics

Most important in the identification portion of this lesson will be those students who are able to complete these activities correctly and independently. Note these students in the appropriate box at the bottom of the *PETS™ Behavioral Checklist - Visual Thinking*. Also note students who discover the pattern to the codes and use that, along with deductive logic, to solve the code.

Creative Cryptography

Students will generally develop three types of codes. A code that is completely random and generally solved by using the code key is the most common type devised by students. Students who work at a higher level may develop a code with a system or pattern such as assigning each letter of the alphabet a number. This code has a definite pattern but may not be unique. Note especially those students who are able to design a code with a system or pattern that works and is unique or subtle.

THE PUZZLERS' CLUB

Dudley the Detective, Sybil the Scientist, and Max the Magician are known throughout Crystal Pond Woods for their convergent thinking abilities. One afternoon, as they sat studying the clouds in the sky, Max had a great idea.

"Dudley! Sybil!" Max said with growing excitement. "Let's start a club for those who are visual as well as convergent thinkers. We could have a special club name and hold meetings! We could share our favorite puzzles with each other."

"That's a great idea!" exclaimed Sybil. "The members could also take turns trying to find the most challenging puzzles to bring to the club meetings."

"Yes!" joined in Dudley. "I can't think of anything more fun than trying to solve challenging puzzles. Let's call our club **THE PUZZLERS' CLUB**."

"That's a great name, Dudley. How should we let the others in the Woods know about our new club?" asked Sybil.

As the three friends thought about it, Max the Magician had a wonderful idea. "Why don't we devise a code? We could use it to write an invitation to the first club meeting! We can use shapes and lines to write the code," he suggested. "Then we know that those who come to the first meeting have already found the answer to the first puzzle."

"I think that's a great idea," enthused Sybil. "Did you know that a code itself is called a **cipher**?" Sybil the Scientist knew lots of scientific words.

"That's a very interesting word," interrupted Dudley.

"I have more words," continued Sybil. "When you rewrite a message in code it is called **encoding**. First, we have to decide what to write for our invitation to the first meeting, then we will have to create a code, and finally, we will write our invitation using the code we created."

"So we will **encode** our invitation," clarified Max. "What is it called when our friends are able to solve the code and read the message?"

"That's called **decoding**. Our friends who come to the first club meeting will have already decoded our first puzzle!" exclaimed Sybil.

The three friends decided that Max the Magician would create the code. The next day, they met at Sybil's laboratory and Max the Magician proudly displayed his encoded invitation.

*(Place **Max's Mystery Message** on the overhead projector. The decoded message is:*

You are invited to the very first meeting of the Puzzlers' Club. Meet at Sybil's lab tomorrow. Puzzle lovers only!

"Let's see if we can figure out the message, Sybil," challenged Dudley.

"Wow," worried Sybil, "it all looks like gibberish to me. I don't know where to start."

Dudley's eyes lit up. "I have an idea," he said thoughtfully. "Notice this apostrophe at the end of a word. It is unusual to have an apostrophe without a letter after it. Usually that happens after an **S**. I'm going to see what happens if I assign an **S** to that symbol."

*(Demonstrate by pointing out the apostrophe in line 4 of **Max's Mystery Message**.)*

"If you are correct," replied Max, "then every symbol like that in the code stands for the letter **S**." Max proceeded to write the letter **S** below each of those symbols.

*(Below each of the **S** symbols, write the letter **S**. The remainder of the story is designed to give students strategies to use when decoding puzzles. The story does not have to be completed; however, the strategies described should be presented to the class.)*

"That makes sense because that means there's an **S** after the second apostrophe which is fairly common," added Sybil.

Sybil and Dudley continued to stare at the coded message. "Oh, look!" exclaimed Sybil. "I recognize my name in the message! See — this word begins with an **S** and it only has five letters in it like my name."

Sybil was correct and Max wrote her name below the symbols.

(Fill in Sybil's name at the appropriate place.)

"Don't you also have to fill in the symbols that we now know stand for **Y**, **B**, **I**, and **L** in the rest of the puzzle?" asked Dudley.

"Yes," replied Max. "That is such an important part of the decoding process that I wanted to see if you would remember to do it!"

(Write the appropriate letters below the symbols in the rest of the code.)

"From one of my classifying activities, I know that **E** is the most commonly used letter of the alphabet. I wonder if the most commonly used symbol in this puzzle could be an **E**?" mused Sybil. "What do you think, Dudley?"

(Ask students which symbol seems to be used most often. Point to the appropriate symbol.)

Dudley looked carefully at the puzzle. "I think you may be right, Sybil," answered Dudley. "I think it is an **E** because I see two places where that letter symbol is doubled, and **E** can be doubled."

Max just smiled and wrote the letter **E** below each of the symbols Dudley had indicated.

Meanwhile, Sybil was working on the rest of the message. "Dudley, I think I recognize a system to this code. Don't you think each symbol sort of looks like the letter it is supposed to be?" Dudley listened to Sybil's logical reasoning and agreed with her. As Max filled in the letters below more symbols, the friends were able to decode the rest of the puzzle.

(Ask students if they can think of a word that begins with the letter I and fits the context of the puzzle. As the puzzle is filled in on the overhead transparency, students will begin to guess the rest of the symbols quickly and correctly. Some students may even notice that the symbols may resemble the letters. After completing and reading the puzzle, finish the story.)

Dudley and Sybil were so excited after decoding Max's puzzle, they decided to devise their own codes for the first meeting of **The Puzzlers' Club**. Can you decode their puzzles?

Max's Mystery Message

From the desk of Max the Magician

1   ▽✻ʊ   ∆ᒋ⊖   ↑Ⴖ▽↑⌐⊖ⴱ

2   ⊥✻   ⊥ᒣ⊖   ▽⊖ᒋ▽   ⟨↑ᒋ⟍⊥

3   ⱕ⊖⊖⊥↑Ⴖ⊖   ✻ᒋ   ⊥ᒣ⊖

4   ꙮʊ◪◪ᒋⵁ⟍'   ⟩⌐ʊ3.

5   ⱕ⊖⊖⊥   ∆⊥   ⟍▽3↑⌐'⟍

6   ⌐∆3   ⊥✻ⱕ✻ᒋᒋ✻ꙮ.

7   ꙮʊ◪◪⌐⊖   ⌐✻▽⊖ᒋⵁ

8   ✻Ⴖ⌐▽ !

Name _____

Sybil's Cipher

Can you decode this message from Sybil?

From the laboratory of Sybil the Scientist

___ ___ ___

___ ___ ___ ___ ___ ___ ___ ___

___ ___ ___ ___ ___ ___ ___ ___ ___

___ ___

___ ___ ___ ___ ___ ___ .

Name _____

Hexagon Hieroglyphics

Can you decode this message from Dudley?

From the office of Dudley the Detective

_ _ _ _ _ G _ _

_ _ _ _ _ _ _ _ _ _ _ _

_ _ _ _ _ _ _ _ _ _ _ _

_ _ _ _ M _ _ _ _ _ _ _ _

_

_ _ _ _ _ ' _ _ _ _ _ B !

Name _____

Creative Cryptography

Design your own code!
Write a cryptogram (or message) for a friend using your cipher.

A	B	C	D	E	F	G	H	I

J	K	L	M	N	O	P	Q	R

S	T	U	V	W	X	Y	Z

VISUAL THINKING
SMALL GROUP
LESSON 1

PURPOSE

The purpose of this lesson is to allow students an opportunity to use visual and convergent thinking as they match pairs of shapes that are rotated in different positions on dominoes.

MATERIALS

— one set of *Rotation Dominoes* per student, each set copied onto a different color of paper
— a copy of *PETS™ Small Group Checklist* for each student

LESSON PLAN

1. Each student will be working with a set of *Rotation Dominoes*. To distinguish the sets easily, copy them onto different colors of paper. The teacher may want to laminate and cut out the dominoes ahead of time.

2. The goal is to arrange the 26 dominoes so that pairs of identical but rotated shapes are matched end to end. (To save space, the *Rotation Dominoes* can be arranged in an oval instead of a straight line.) Students are to study the shapes, rotate them in their minds, and find the matching pairs. When all shapes have been correctly matched, the first domino on one end will match the last domino on the other end. Should errors occur anywhere in the sequence, have students study their matches to find and correct the errors.

3. Use pentominoes as an extension activity.

DIAGNOSTIC NOTES

Look for students who are able to find and use a strategy. Instead of looking for the "right" shape one at a time, students might match pairs as they are found, linking pairs to make trains. Look for students who quickly realize that reversing a train is sometimes necessary to make a match. Timing the completion of this activity is important. Look for students who instinctively know the opposite ends of their chain will match before the chain is completed. Also look for students who complete this activity rapidly and just cannot resist "explaining" rotations to others.

Rotation Dominoes

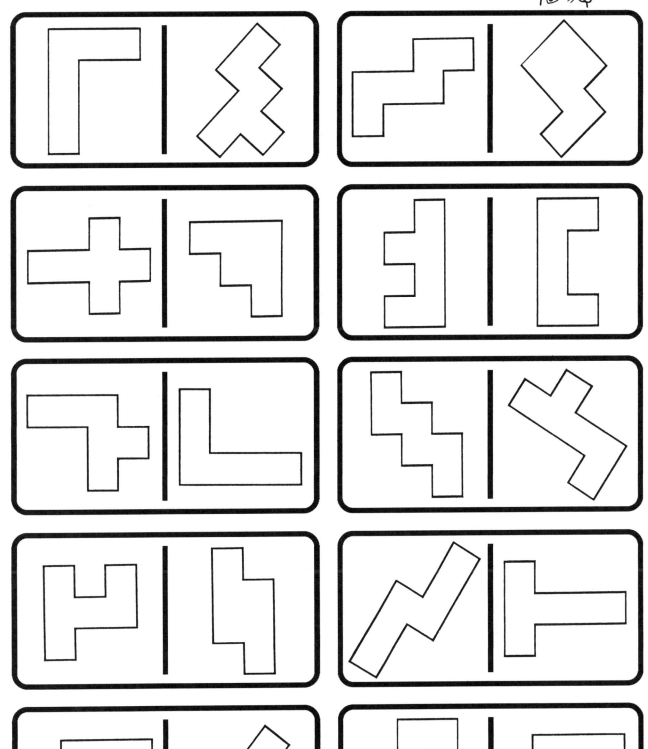

Rotation Dominoes

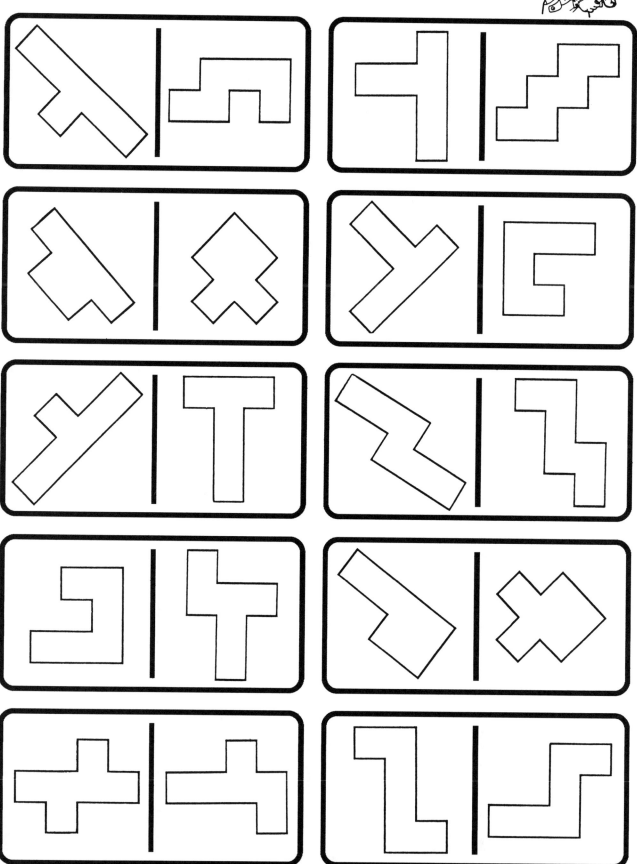

Rotation Dominoes

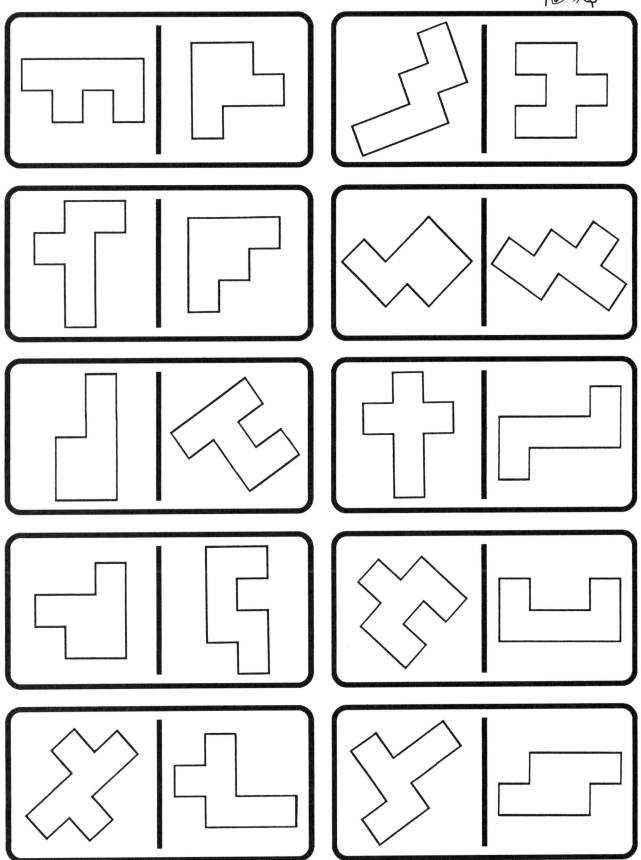

VISUAL THINKING
SMALL GROUP
LESSON 2

The purpose of this lesson is to provide students with an opportunity to use visual, convergent, and divergent thinking as they develop strategies for the game *Think Ahead!*

— duplicated copies of the game *Think Ahead!*
— a copy of *PETS™ Small Group Checklist* for each student

1. *Think Ahead!* is a strategy game in which students must think several moves ahead in order to box in a geometric shape or shapes and claim ownership of that shape.

2. Read aloud to students the following rules for *Think Ahead!*

— Students take turns drawing one line on the grid. A line goes from one bold dot to the next bold dot along the dotted path.
— When a student "boxes in" a shape, he or she claims it by writing his or her initial in that shape or shapes.
— After claiming a shape, the student must continue play by adding one line to the grid, even if it means that his or her opponent can now claim a shape.
— Play continues until all shapes are claimed.

3. Students need to play the game several times against various opponents in order to develop and test winning strategies.

4. Capable students who enjoy the thinking strategies in *Think Ahead!* may want to design their own game boards. A change in the design changes the strategies involved in playing the game. The inclusion of a variety of polygons and the way they are arranged make the game interesting.

DIAGNOSTIC NOTES

Look for students whose strategies allow them to win consistently. These students are devising more sophisticated strategies as they play the game.

Look for students who, when they realize their opponent will earn a shape, seek to minimize losses by drawing a line where it will give up the fewest shapes.

There is a "cascading effect," especially near the end of the game, when one completed shape allows many shapes to be completed. Look for students who use this "cascading effect" in their winning strategy.

Note students who show flexibility of thought in the creation of unique strategies.

Note students who enjoy the complex thinking processes involved in playing *Think Ahead!* and who play aggressively. It is easier to see the students who do not display this characteristic; they play the game by only reacting to their opponents' moves.

Note those students who design creative, usable game boards and are able to analyze the strategies necessary to win the game they create.

NOTES

Think Ahead!

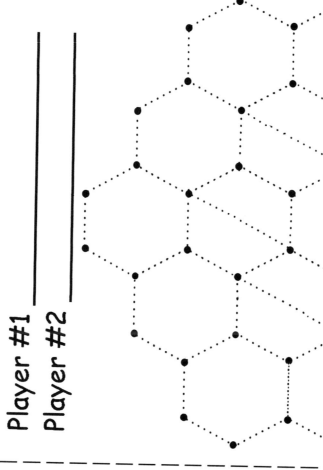

Player #1 _____
Player #2 _____

✂ -

Think Ahead!

Player #1 _____
Player #2 _____

142

VISUAL THINKING
SMALL GROUP
LESSON 3

PURPOSE

The purpose of this lesson is to provide students with an opportunity to develop their visual reasoning as they identify and name figural attributes.

MATERIALS

- one blue paper circle with a 24" diameter
- one red paper circle with a 16" diameter
- a *Name the Club* attribute deck for each student
- a duplicated copy of *The Club Rule* for each hand played
- a copy of *PETS™ Small Group Checklist* for each student

LESSON PLAN

1. To prepare the *Name the Club* game board, glue the red paper circle in the center of the blue circle. To distinguish each set of *Name the Club* decks easily, copy them on different colors of paper or card stock. Teachers may want to laminate the decks for use year after year.

2. Give each student a different colored *Name the Club* deck. Have students place the deck in front of them with the cards face up and outside the game board.

3. The Club Leader decides on a rule (attribute) which will determine membership into the Club. (Color cannot be used as an attribute.) For example, the Club Leader may decide the rule is "cards with a triangle." The rule is written on *The Club Rule* card and slid under the game board. The teacher may want to serve as the Club Leader for the first round to model the process. The Club Leader is responsible for all decisions concerning membership in the Club as well as revealing *The Club Rule* when the Club is correctly identified. The teacher may want to read *The Club Rule* when written by students so s/he can monitor the correct play of the game.

4. The student to the left of the Club Leader begins play by selecting one card from his or her *Name the Club* deck and asking the Club Leader if the card belongs in the Club. If the answer is "yes," the card is placed on the red circle of the playing board. If the answer is "no," it is placed on the blue circle.

5. Play continues clockwise as each student has the option of either offering a card for Club membership or naming the Club, but not both in one turn. If a student offers a card that has already been played by another student, he or she loses that turn.

6. Should the teacher wish to keep score, the player who correctly names the Club scores five points. In addition, all students earn one point for each card from their deck that is a member of the Club.

7. After scoring is completed, collect all cards and return them to the proper decks and play begins again. The student who correctly named the previous Club becomes the new Club Leader.

8. If a Club has not been named in three rounds of questioning, the Club Leader scores five points and must explain the rule. The player to his or her left then becomes the new Club Leader.

DIAGNOSTIC NOTES

Look for students who can recognize attributes and deduce the shared figural attribute that names the Club.

Students who study the cards on the blue ring, using the incorrect thinking of other players as a "no" clue, show potential in their visual reasoning.

Watch for students who develop a strategy such as turning over used cards or sorting by attributes. Correctly naming the Club involves a more complex thinking process as the student sorts, rules out, and then deduces the one attribute shared by all cards in the Club.

NOTES

Name the Club

Name the Club

The Club Rule	The Club Rule
The Club Rule	The Club Rule
The Club Rule	The Club Rule
The Club Rule	The Club Rule

PETS

	Behavioral Checklist ---------- Evaluative Thinking	

List names of students as each behavior appears.
   Add checkmarks after name if behavior is repeated.
   Use a different color of ink or pencil for each whole group lesson.
		Teacher _____
		Grade: 1 ___ 2 ___ 3 ___
		
		Date of whole 1. _____
		group instruction 2. _____
		                3. _____

GRASPS CONCEPTS VERY QUICKLY	**DRAWS VALID CONCLUSIONS BASED UPON CRITERIA** DEVELOPED IN THE LESSON
LOGICALLY SUPPORTS RESPONSES	**SEES MORE THAN ONE VIEWPOINT**
OFFERS UNIQUE SOLUTIONS AND/OR **CRITERIA**	**DISPLAYS LONG ATTENTION SPAN** - WORKS EXERCISE DILIGENTLY TO THE END
PETS classwork indicates an outstanding ability to use this thinking skill.	The following student/s did not participate during the thinking skills lessons, but I see these behaviors during regular class time.

In this unit, students are introduced to the concepts of criterion-based evaluative thinking. Evaluative thinking is necessary in many daily activities and is a vital part of the problem-solving process so critical to the 21st century. In this type of thinking, students seek the best solution based on factual criteria. Within a story setting, Jordan the Judge utilizes this type of thinking as he helps students from Crystal Pond School develop factual criteria, as well as when he partners his thinking skill with those of Isabel the Inventor and Max the Magician in two activities which encourage the application of factual criteria in the decision-making process.

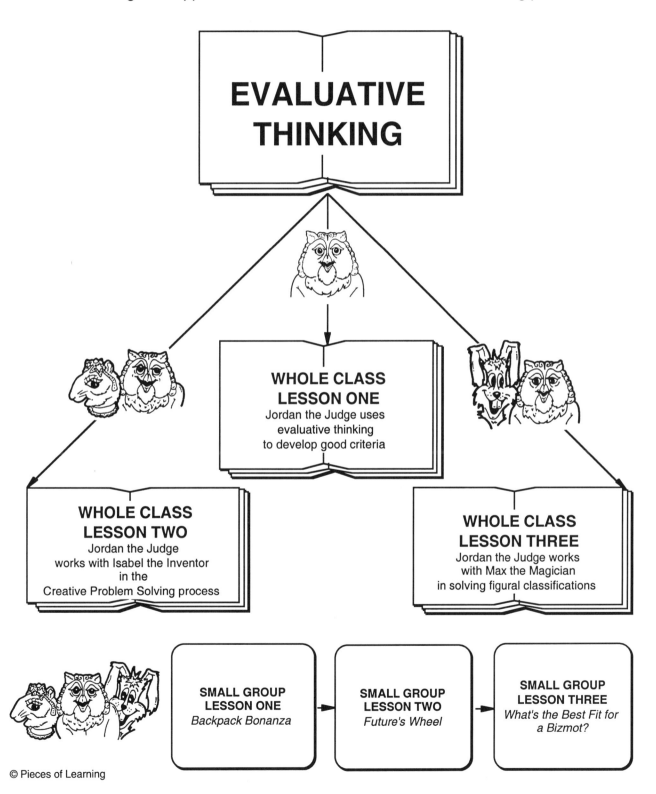

EVALUATIVE THINKING

WHOLE CLASS LESSON ONE
Jordan the Judge uses evaluative thinking to develop good criteria

WHOLE CLASS LESSON TWO
Jordan the Judge works with Isabel the Inventor in the Creative Problem Solving process

WHOLE CLASS LESSON THREE
Jordan the Judge works with Max the Magician in solving figural classifications

SMALL GROUP LESSON ONE
Backpack Bonanza

SMALL GROUP LESSON TWO
Future's Wheel

SMALL GROUP LESSON THREE
What's the Best Fit for a Bizmot?

Evaluative Thinking

EVALUATIVE THINKING
WHOLE CLASS
LESSON 1

PURPOSE

The purpose of this lesson is to reinforce the concepts of criterion-based evaluative thinking. The emphasis is the development of good factual criteria necessary to judge multiple solutions.

MATERIALS

— a copy of the story *A School Improvement Plan*
— an overhead transparency of *School Improvements*
— an overhead transparency of *Birthday Banquet*
— a board or chart paper to record student suggestions for criteria
— a duplicated class set of *Car-Buying Criteria*
— *PETS™ Behavioral Checklist - Evaluative Thinking*

LESSON PLAN

1. It is important to give students a chance to review the three types of thinking developed so far: convergent, divergent, and visual. Students should be able to verbalize characteristics of the types of thinking as well as when the various types of thinking might be used.

2. If students have completed **PRIMARY EDUCATION THINKING SKILLS I,** they learned about *thinking like a judge.* This is *evaluative thinking,* and students will need to be introduced to the term. Review with students the main points of evaluative thinking:

— Decisions are based on valid, factual considerations rather than opinions.
— From among many choices, criteria can help guide students to the best solution.

3. Read the story *A School Improvement Plan* aloud to students. The main points of the story are that criteria are standards or facts on which judgments can be based and that these criteria need to be observable or measurable.

4. As a class, practice developing criteria using the scenario *Birthday Banquet*. List the criteria developed on the board. Encourage the class to come up with several criteria and ways to measure or observe the criteria, even if that measurement is impractical for the students to implement. Be sure to accept any reasonable, valid criteria. Do not restrict the class to pre-conceived ideas of what makes a good rule of measure, and do not try to steer them toward any one idea.

5. As students suggest criterion ideas, the teacher should phrase the statement in a desirable, measurable direction. For example:

Student: I'd like a restaurant that is near my home.
Teacher: Which is <u>the closest restaurant</u> to your home?
Student: I want a restaurant where the people are friendly.
Teacher: Which has <u>the friendliest staff</u>?

CHALLENGE PAGE

Car-Buying Criteria

6. Distribute *Car-Buying Criteria* to students. Completion of this page will allow the teacher an opportunity to see which students understand the development of factual criteria.

DIAGNOSTIC NOTES

The following is a short summary of what to look for in student behaviors and responses for Evaluative Thinking, Whole Class 1:

GRASPS CONCEPTS VERY QUICKLY - Look for students who are able to develop <u>factual</u>, <u>measurable</u> criteria. Note students who can demonstrate fluency in their list of criterion ideas.

CAN LOGICALLY SUPPORT RESPONSES - Look for students who can support criteria by offering ways of observing or measuring the criteria. These students may be able to convince the teacher their rationale is sound despite initial doubts.

OFFERS UNIQUE SOLUTIONS AND/OR CRITERIA - Look for students who can produce <u>valid</u> yet creative criteria. These considerations may even surprise the teacher.

DRAWS VALID CONCLUSIONS BASED UPON CRITERIA - Look for students who can accurately apply valid criteria in order to help narrow the field of many choices regardless of their own personal preferences. There will be more opportunity for this in later lessons, but some students may begin to show the understanding of this right away.

SEES MORE THAN ONE VIEWPOINT - Look for students who are able to see another's viewpoint. Especially notable are any students who are able to develop their own valid, factual criteria from the other viewpoint.

DISPLAYS A LONG ATTENTION SPAN - In addition to a long attention span, look for students who want to work on evaluative-type activities. This is the most difficult thinking strategy. Note those students who stick with it and possibly continue to think about it after the session. An enthusiasm towards this type of thinking usually indicates an ability to use it.

Car-Buying Criteria

Look for students who are able to develop good, factual criteria independently. Some acceptable answers are: fits the budget, good gas mileage, and holds six people. By giving students a chance to work independently, the teacher should see a difference between those students who understand the concept of factual criteria and those who are still adding "I like it" as a criterion. Students are not expected to write directional criteria independently so it is important to note those who do.

NOTES

A SCHOOL
IMPROVEMENT PLAN

In Crystal Pond Woods, Jordan the Judge is a careful thinker. He considers all the facts before he makes a decision. His wisdom is so well respected that whenever a difficult or important decision has to be made, the residents of Crystal Pond Woods ask Jordan to help them make the best choice.

On this particular day, Jordan was napping in his hollow at the top of the tallest oak tree when he heard the school bell ring, dismissing the students for the day. Soon the sounds of laughter and shouting could be heard as the children ran from the building and hurried off to play. However, very quickly, students from Crystal Pond School found their way to Jordan's oak tree and shouted for him to come out to hear their problem.

Jordan hopped onto a limb not too far above the children. "Whooo is it that needs my help?" he asked in a dignified voice.

One girl, Alice, stepped forward. "Your Honor," she said, "something very exciting has happened at Crystal Pond School! An anonymous donation of $1200.00 has been made to the school, and Ms. Jennings, the principal, has asked the Student Council for help in determining how the money should be spent."

"I see," replied Jordan. "You are right. That is indeed very exciting. Has Ms. Jennings made any suggestions for how it might be spent?"

"Yes," answered Alice. "We all helped her think of ideas today at our Student Council meeting." Alice held out the list of ideas for Jordan to see.

*(Place **School Improvements** on the overhead projector and read the list aloud to the class.)*

Jordan was impressed. "These are very admirable suggestions," he told the children. "What can I do to help?"

"We can't decide which idea is the **best** one," Alice explained. "Some people like one idea and others like another. We need an **objective** way to figure out which idea is the best."

"I see," said Jordan. "What you need are some good **criteria** by which you can judge your ideas."

"What are criteria?" asked Bill, a boy from the group.

"Criteria are rules or standards on which judgments can be based. They work best if they are observable or measurable by everyone in the same way. In simpler terms, they are the **facts we need to consider when we make an important decision**. As I am thinking, I ask myself, 'What are the considerations?' For this particular problem you may want to consider what most of the people affected by this decision would like."

"That makes sense," Bill declared, "so our best choice would be the one that **will please the most students**."

"That's a good criterion," approved Jordan. "Is it measurable?"

"Sure," said Alice. "We could take a survey of the students to find out what they like."

"Good," responded Jordan, writing down the criterion. "When making your decision, it should please the most students."

(Write the label **Criteria** *on the board and add* **"Which will please the most students?"** *as the first of the list of criteria.)*

"What other facts do you think you need to consider when you make this choice?" inquired Jordan.

(The remainder of the story models the process of developing the factual criteria needed to make a good decision. A teacher may choose to do this without finishing the story by having the class brainstorm its own criteria.)

"I think that we have to consider the safety of the students," said Bob, joining in the discussion.

"How would we measure safety?" questioned Alice.

"My dad is a fireman," Bill replied. "Maybe he could look over our list and tell us which ideas are safe ideas and which ones are unsafe."

Jordan added **Which is safest for students?** to his list.

(Add to the list on the board.)

"We might want to consider something that will last a long time," suggested Mary.

"That's a good idea," replied Alice. "We could add **Which will be the longest lasting?**"

(Add to the list on the board.)

"Gym is my favorite class! I like the idea of getting new gym equipment with the money!" exclaimed Bill.

"Liking something is an opinion," responded Jordan. "When developing criteria, we want to base them on facts. Maybe we can rephrase Bill's idea so it can be based on measurable or observable facts. What is it that you **like** about gym equipment?"

"Well, I use the gym equipment every day. So do my classmates. I think we should get something that is the **most often used**," answered Bill.

*(Encourage students to phrase the question "**Which will be most often used?**")*

"You know, if we keep these questions, or criteria, in mind when considering this whole list of ideas, they can really help us narrow our choices so that we'll be able to make the best choice! This is great!" realized Alice. "Thank you, Your Honor, so much for your ideas. We'll take this list of criteria to the Student Council meeting tomorrow!"

"I'm so glad I was able to help," replied Jordan the Judge. "The Student Council may have additional criteria to add to the list. Happy decision making!"

And with that, Jordan the Judge flew back up to the hollow of his oak tree and resumed his nap.

School Improvements

1. Improvements to the cafeteria area

2. New playground equipment

3. New equipment for the learning center or media center

4. Divide the amount equally between the classrooms for individual use

5. New gym equipment

6. Donate the entire amount to a special charity

7. Updated equipment in the school office

8. Improved lighting for the stage in the auditorium

9. Twelve new lockers to replace old broken ones

10. All-school field trip to an amusement park

Birthday Banquet

Alice and her sisters cannot decide where to take their mother for a special dinner on her birthday. Alice wants to avoid an argument. Remembering what she has been learning from Jordan the Judge, Alice tells her sisters that factual, observable criteria will help them make the best choice. What are some criteria they might use?

Where to take Mom for a birthday banquet?

Which restaurant ... ??

1.

2.

3.

4.

5.

6.

7.

8.

Name _____

Car-Buying Criteria

Your family has decided to buy a new car! Your parents have asked you to help in making this very important decision. You know that cars are a big purchase and that much thought goes into the decision. What factual, observable criteria would you use to help your parents make up their minds?

A car that...

A car that...

A car that...

A car that...

A car that...

EVALUATIVE THINKING
WHOLE CLASS
LESSON 2

PURPOSE

The purpose of this lesson is to introduce the creative problem-solving process. The emphasis is on the use of factual criteria to determine the best solution when there is a choice to be made.

MATERIALS

- a copy of the story *What's Best for Crystal Pond School?*
- an overhead transparency of *The Problem-Solving Matrix*
- an overhead transparency of *What's Best for Our School?*
- an overhead transparency of *Max's Mess*
- a duplicated class set of *Max's Mess*
- a duplicated class set of *Chow Time!*
- *PETS™ Behavioral Checklist - Evaluative Thinking*

LESSON PLAN

1. Review with students the main points of evaluative thinking:
   - Decisions are based on valid, factual criteria, not opinions.
   - From among many choices, criteria can help guide students to the best solution.

2. Read the story *What's Best for Crystal Pond School?* aloud to the students. The main point of the story is that criteria make it possible to evaluate possible solutions to a problem in such a way that one "best" solution can be determined. Other points include:

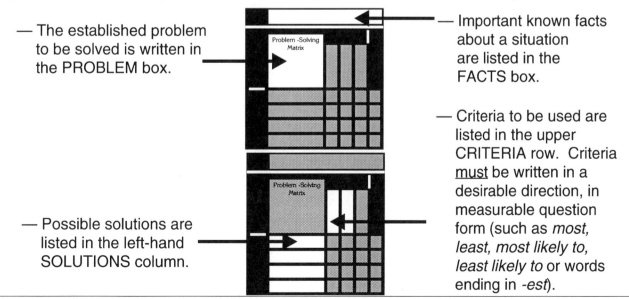

- The established problem to be solved is written in the PROBLEM box.

- Important known facts about a situation are listed in the FACTS box.

- Criteria to be used are listed in the upper CRITERIA row. Criteria <u>must</u> be written in a desirable direction, in measurable question form (such as *most, least, most likely to, least likely to* or words ending in *-est*).

- Possible solutions are listed in the left-hand SOLUTIONS column.

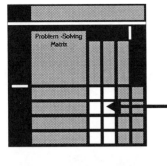

— Problem-solving matrices have rows and columns that criss-cross to create cells.

— Solutions are ranked according to each listed criterion from one (low) to the number reflecting the total of possible solutions (high). For example, if there were five possible solutions, they would be ranked from one to five.

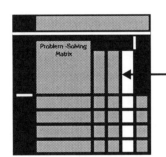

Sometimes it may not seem possible to rate solutions differentially. Nonetheless, they <u>must</u> be ranked somehow — each column may only contain <u>one</u> of each number.

— Each row is totaled <u>across</u>, putting the total in the right-hand SCORING COLUMN.

The solution with the highest score is the best solution given these particular criteria.

Students may justifiably disagree on how to rank solutions. When this happens, they will end up with different "best" solutions. This is fine as long as they can justify their rankings.

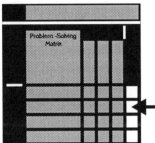

— If two or more solutions tie with the highest score, the shaded Tie-Breaker Column is used. Create another criterion, rate and rank the solutions, and re-total the rows.

3. As a class, practice the creative problem-solving process using *Max's Mess*. Have students work the problem individually following the teacher's demonstration. Students need to brainstorm three more possible solutions and one more criterion. Possible solutions are: *sort things into labeled containers, sort things into piles, hire a cleaning person, dig a bigger burrow in order to spread things out more*. Possible criteria include: *can be accomplished quickest, costs the least*. Add these to the overhead transparency. Since there are five possible solutions, rank them from one to five.

While most students will need to follow the teacher's demonstration, allow those students who are ready to brainstorm their own solutions and criteria as well as establish their own rankings to do so. Note those students who grasp these concepts quickly on the *PETS™ Behavioral Checklist*. Tell students that either approach is acceptable.

CHALLENGE PAGE

Chow Time!

4. Distribute *Chow Time!* to students. If students need a jump-start, brainstorm as a class possible criteria for choosing the best place to eat before starting the Challenge Page.

DIAGNOSTIC NOTES

The following is a short summary of what to look for in student behaviors and responses for Evaluative Thinking, Whole Class 2:

GRASPS CONCEPTS VERY QUICKLY - Look for students who are quickly able to understand and to use the creative problem-solving process. Note students whose criteria are not only valid, but also appropriately directional and indicate a measure of degree. List students who are the first to determine a best solution.

CAN LOGICALLY SUPPORT RESPONSES - Look for students who state opinions and can follow up their opinions with logical reasoning. Watch for this when solutions are being ranked.

OFFERS UNIQUE SOLUTIONS AND/OR CRITERIA - Look for students who offer valid solutions and/or criteria that may not be directly from or related to the story or scenario.

DRAWS VALID CONCLUSIONS BASED UPON CRITERIA - Look for students who can effectively evaluate and rank possible solutions by applying the criteria, thereby deriving a valid best solution.

SEES MORE THAN ONE VIEWPOINT - Look for students who are able to see the problem from another's perspective. These students may also understand how the best solution may vary from person to person.

DISPLAYS A LONG ATTENTION SPAN - In addition to a long attention span, look for students who want to work on evaluative thinking activities. An enthusiasm towards this type of thinking may indicate a talent for it.

Max's Mess and *Chow Time!*

Note those students who are able to use the creative problem-solving matrix correctly and can complete it independently. Look for those students who not only generate unique solutions and criteria but are already able to phrase the criteria correctly as well.

WHAT'S BEST FOR CRYSTAL POND SCHOOL?

High up in the branches of the tallest oak tree in Crystal Pond Woods, Jordan the Judge was telling Isabel the Inventor about the Crystal Pond School Student Council's dilemma. He was explaining how the school had received a donation of $1200. He told her how the students had brainstormed a list of criteria for evaluating their long list of possible school improvements. While they were chatting the sounds of student voices began to filter through the woodland stillness.

"Your Honor!" called Bill. "We need your help!" Jordan and Isabel both peered down at the students from the Student Council who had gathered below.

"We have the list of school improvements and the list of criteria," continued Alice. "We've narrowed our list of choices, but we don't know how to use these criteria to end up with just one solution that is best for our school."

Isabel nudged Jordan. "Sounds to me like they need to use a creative problem-solving matrix. Don't you agree, Jordan?"

"I think you're absolutely right, Isabel," said Jordan, and the two friends descended to the forest floor and gathered the children around them. Jordan drew a matrix on the ground for the children to view.

*(Place **The Problem-Solving Matrix** on the overhead projector.)*

"Why, that looks a lot like Dudley's logic elimination grid!" exclaimed Bill. "Does it work the same way?"

"Not really," Jordan responded, "so let's go over the different parts of this matrix. In the **FACTS** box, it's important to list the actual facts that you know about your situation. The problem that you want to solve is then posed in the **PROBLEM** box. This column here is for a list of possible solutions, while over there is where you would list things you need to consider when rating your solutions. In other words, these are your criteria. These other cells are where you will rate each of your solutions using each of your criteria."

"Wow," sighed Mary, "that looks awfully complicated. Are you sure it'll help us?"

"Absolutely," assured both Jordan and Isabel. "Now let's consider your situation," continued Jordan.

"First let's make sure we agree on the facts and just what the problem is that you want to solve. We'll need to write those down clearly in the matrix."

"That's easy," answered Alice. "One fact is that our school was given $1200."

"And another," chimed in Bill, "is that our school needs lots of improvements."

"So let's write that information into the **FACTS** box like this," showed Jordan.

*(Place **What's Best for Our School?** on the overhead projector. Point out the two facts written in the **FACTS** box.)*

"We also already know what our problem is," offered Mary, catching on. "We need to decide what is the best school improvement that can be made with the money that was donated. I'll write that in the **PROBLEM** box, okay?"

*(Point out the problem written in the **PROBLEM** box.)*

"That's great," encouraged Isabel. "Now Jordan has just been telling me how you've already brainstormed a great list of needed school improvements. Brainstorming is my favorite part of creative problem-solving, you know. And I see that you've already narrowed that list down to the five possibilities that you feel are probably your best choices. Let's list them in the **SOLUTIONS** column like this."

*(Point out and read the possible solutions that have been listed in the **SOLUTIONS** column.)*

"Isabel, they also brainstormed a fine list of criteria for judging these possible solutions," spoke up Jordan. "You would have been very proud of them. Those should be listed in the **CRITERIA** row like this."

*(Point out and read the criteria listed in the **CRITERIA** column.)*

"Now," announced Jordan, "we're all ready to rate your solutions using your criteria. We'll start with which of these five solutions **will please the most students**. We're going to rate them from one to five, since there are five solutions. One will be the solution that pleases the least number of students and five will be the solution that will please the most students. Didn't you do a student survey to find this out?"

"Yes, we did," answered Alice. "We found out that most of the students want to go on an all-school field trip to the amusement park. The smallest number of students want new stage lighting. More students want new playground equipment than want either new lockers or to divide up the money between the different classes. More students want new lockers than class money."

"In that case," continued Jordan, "we'll give the field trip a 5 in the cell it shares with this criterion. *(Put a 5 in the cell that field trip shares with **Will please the most students**.)* Then we'll put a 1 in the cell that goes with stage lighting, a 4 in the cell that goes with playground equipment, a 2 in the cell that goes with dividing the money between classes and a 3 in the cell that goes with new lockers. *(Put the numbers in the appropriate cells on the overhead transparency.)* Now we have rated each of your solutions for this one criterion. Let's move on to the next criterion: Which solution **will last the longest**? What did you find out about this?"

"We checked out the warrantees on the equipment," reported Mary. "While new lockers should last 15 years and new stage lighting for 10 years, new playground equipment is only expected to last for 5 years. New classroom materials will get used up during the year, and the field trip is only good for one day!"

"That means that for this criterion," Bill was busily figuring, "new lockers gets the 5 and the field trip gets the 1. New stage lighting gets the 4, while divide the money gets the 2, and new playground equipment gets the 3, right?"

(Demonstrate by writing the numbers in the appropriate cells of the grid.)

"Exactly," approved Jordan. "I think you're ready to continue to rate these solutions according to the other two criteria by yourself."

(As a class, rate the solutions using the remaining two criteria, and fill in the cells accordingly.)

"We finished!" declared the children finally. "What's next?"

"Now we add up each row of numbers from left to right and put the total for each row in the cell that row shares with the **SCORING COLUMN** on the far right," instructed Jordan.

(Add up each row of four numbers and put the total in the row's ***SCORING COLUMN*** *cell.)*

"Then look," continued Jordan, for this was the part he liked the best, "for the solution with the highest score and circle it, because, given these criteria, that, my young friends, is your best solution."

(The story ends here unless two or more solutions tie with the highest score. In that case, continue reading.)

"But, Your Honor," Alice sounded very concerned, "there's a tie between these solutions. Their scores are all the highest. What do we do now?"

"That's the purpose of this shaded column here," explained Jordan. "It's the **Tie-Breaker Column**. We'll just add another criterion there, rate the solutions again, and re-total any ties. Try it."

(Add another criterion in the shaded ***Tie-Breaker Column***. *Rate the solutions. Re-add the rows and determine the solution with the highest score.)*

The Problem-Solving Matrix

FACTS	the facts of the situation

Problem-Solving Matrix | **CRITERIA** | SCORING COLUMN

PROBLEM	the problem that must be solved	things to be considered when a choice must be made	
SOLUTIONS	the possible solutions		where solutions get rated & ranked

What's Best for Our School?

1. Someone donated $1200 to Crystal Pond School.
2. The school needs a lot of improvements.

Problem-Solving Matrix	CRITERIA					SCORING COLUMN
PROBLEM — What's the best school improvement that can be made with the money that was donated to Crystal Pond School?	Will please the most students?	Will be the most long lasting?	Will be safest for the students?	Will be used most frequently?		
SOLUTIONS New playground equipment						
Twelve new lockers						
New stage lighting						
Divide money between classes						
All-school field trip to amusement park						

Matrix©Dodie Merritt

Name _____

Max's Mess

FACTS
1. Max likes to collect all kinds of things for his magic shows.
2. Things are piled up all through his burrow.
3. He does not even know everything he has!

Problem-Solving Matrix | CRITERIA

PROBLEM		Will keep burrow neat the longest?	Will be easiest to keep on doing?	Most likely to keep special things from being lost by mistake?		SCORING COLUMN
What's the best plan that will help Max keep his burrow neatly organized?						
SOLUTIONS	1. Throw everything out					
	2. Make an alphabetical list					
	3.					
	4.					
	5.					

Matrix©Dodie Merritt

Name _____

Chow Time!

It's Friday night.
Everyone in your family is tired from work or from school.
Everyone in your family is very hungry.
It's your turn to choose the restaurant where your family will eat dinner.

PROBLEM

Problem-Solving Matrix

CRITERIA

What's the best place
for your family to go
for dinner?

Write 4 criteria that will help
you choose the best place to go
and eat. List them in this row.

List 4 or 5 favorite restaurants
below in this column.

SCORING COLUMN

	1.	2.	3.	4.	
SOLUTIONS					
1.					
2.					
3.					
4.					
5.					

Matrix©Dodie Merritt

EVALUATIVE THINKING
WHOLE CLASS
LESSON 3

PURPOSE

The purpose of this lesson is to combine evaluative thinking and visual thinking. The use of good factual criteria to judge multiple solutions will be reinforced.

MATERIALS

— a copy of the story *Card Sharks*
— an overhead transparency of *Jordan's Cards 1* and *2*
— an overhead transparency of *Jordan's Cards 3* and *4*
— a duplicated class set of *Quintessential Sets 1*
— a duplicated class set of *Quintessential Sets 2*
— *PETS™ Behavioral Checklist - Evaluative Thinking*

LESSON PLAN

1. Review with students the main points of evaluative thinking:
   — Decisions are based on valid, factual criteria, not opinions.
   — From among many choices, criteria can help guide students to the best solution.

2. Read the story *Card Sharks* aloud to students. The main points of the story include:
   — Criteria must be applied to arrive at the best solution.
   — Multiple criteria are effective at narrowing the field of choices.
   — When different criteria are applied to the same problem, the solution may be different.

CHALLENGE PAGES

Quintessential Sets 1   *Quintessential Sets 2*

3. Distribute *Quintessential Sets 1* and *Quintessential Sets 2* to students. They will be practicing the skills developed during the lesson. Each page has three sets and the sets increase in difficulty. If some students choose not to finish because of the difficulty of the work, allow them to turn in as much as they were able to accomplish.
Possible answers for *Quintessential Sets 1* include but are not limited to:

top set   solution-button up shirt, criterion - clothes that button
           solution-long sleeve turtleneck, criterion - clothes with long sleeves
middle   solution-sponge, criterion - things with holes
set   solution-softball, criterion - things that are round
           solution-thread spool, criterion - things that are round and have a
                                          hole through the center

bottom set   solution-cake, criterion- foods that have a round shape
               solution-cheese, criterion - food that is healthy
               solution-stamp, criterion - things you peel
(Using a criterion such as *food* or *snacks* does not eliminate all but one answer.)

Possible answers for *Quintessential Sets 2* include but are not limited to:

top set   solution-card 3, criterion - shapes that overlap and have a diamond
               solution-card 1, criterion - overlapping shapes with black shape in
                                  shared area
middle set   solution-milk carton, criterion - container
               solution-jack o'lantern, criterion - things without lids
bottom set   solution-card 3, criterion - white circle in white area of shape
               solution-card 1, criterion - completes a sequence as the shape is
                                  darkened

DIAGNOSTIC NOTES

The following is a short summary of what to look for in student behaviors and responses for Evaluative Thinking, Whole Class 3:

GRASPS CONCEPTS VERY QUICKLY - Look for students who are able to develop <u>factual</u>, <u>measurable</u> criteria and demonstrate fluency in their list of criterion ideas. Note students who can quickly apply criteria to determine the best solution.

CAN LOGICALLY SUPPORT RESPONSES - Capable students can state the criteria used in determining their selections.

OFFERS UNIQUE SOLUTIONS AND/OR CRITERIA - Look for students who offer relevant but unusual criteria for determining their choices.

DRAWS VALID CONCLUSIONS BASED UPON CRITERIA - Look for students who can accurately apply valid criteria in order to help narrow the field of many choices regardless of their own personal preferences.

SEES MORE THAN ONE VIEWPOINT - Look for students who are able to see the issue from another's perspective. These students may also understand how the decision may be different depending on the criteria used to make the selection.

DISPLAYS A LONG ATTENTION SPAN - In addition to a long attention span, look for students who want to work on evaluative-type activities. An enthusiasm towards this type of thinking often indicates an ability to use it.

Quintessential Sets 1 and *2*
Note students who finish the challenge pages independently, particularly the more difficult items at the end, and can express the criteria validating their selections. Look for student-generated criteria that successfully eliminate all but one possible solution.

CARD SHARKS

It was a rainy afternoon in Crystal Pond Woods, and Max the Magician was bored with his tricks. He had practiced his rope tricks, his hat tricks, and his card tricks, and now he felt restless. He decided to go upstairs in the hollow oak and visit his friend, Jordan the Judge.

Jordan was pleased to see Max, although this dark, rainy day was perfect for taking an afternoon nap. Jordan was not surprised that his rabbit friend felt bored, and he quickly suggested a game of cards. "I'm tired of cards," Max replied.

"This card game is new," Jordan told him, "and it will require a great deal of thought."

"That's more like it!" Max quickly agreed. "My brain could use a work-out!"

Jordan pulled out his deck of cards. They had pictures on them. He laid three cards on the table so Max could see the pictures. Then he laid five more cards on the table in a row below the first group. "Which one of these cards do you think best goes with this first group?" asked Jordan.

*(Place **Jordan's Cards 1** on the overhead projector.)*

Max looked puzzled. The top row of cards showed pictures of Dudley the Detective, Max, and Isabel the Inventor. The second row of cards included Belinda Butterfly, Yolanda the Yarnspinner, Jordan the Judge, Sybil the Scientist, and Petey Parrot. Any of these seemed to be a good choice to him.

"What's going on?" Max asked. "This first group shows animals who live in Crystal Pond Woods and are friends. This second group shows more animals who live in Crystal Pond Woods and are friends. How can I choose the one <u>best</u> card?"

Jordan smiled. "You're right, Max. They all do seem like good choices. But remember, I asked for the <u>best</u> choice. They are all animals. They do all live in Crystal Pond Woods. They are all friends. But that does not help us discriminate among the answer choices. So let's think of other criteria to use. What else do the first pictures have in common that some of the answer choices do not have?"

"I'm stumped," said Max. "They all look equally good to me."

"Not really," replied Jordan. "You, Dudley, and Isabel are all mammals. You wear those fuzzy fur coats. I do not. Yolanda does not. In fact, only one of the possible answer cards is a mammal."

(It may help students if the eliminated cards are crossed out.)

"Sybil!" shouted Max.

"Exactly," agreed Jordan. "Her card is the best solution from the selections you have. You should choose her card to complete the set."

"I think I get it now," said Max. "Let's try again."

Jordan dealt out a new set of cards. *(Place **Jordan's Cards 2** on the overhead projector.)* This set included a frog, a penguin, and a walrus. The answer cards included a choice of a kitten, a squirrel, a cow, an owl like Jordan, and a turtle. Max began to think out loud.

"Let's see...a frog, a penguin, and a walrus are all animals, and so are all my answer choices. That can't be the right criterion to use. The penguin is a bird and so is the owl, but none of the other cards in the first group are birds. What do they **all** have in common? *(Ask the class to volunteer ideas before continuing.)* I know!! A frog, a penguin, and a walrus all live in or near the water. The <u>best</u> choice from the selections I have would be the turtle, right?"

"You're quick to catch on," Jordan smiled. "You figured it out right away." Jordan dealt again. *(Place **Jordan's Cards 3** on the overhead projector.)*

"OK, here goes," said Jordan. He laid out the three set cards. They included a TV set, a bed, and a round table. The answer choices included a chick, a bee, a worm, a fish, and a Great Dane.

"Just when I think I'm getting it," said Max, "you throw one at me that makes no sense at all! How can these animals make a set with those pieces of furniture? That's impossible!"

Jordan sighed. "You just need to think of more criteria, Max. Maybe it is not the fact that they are animals and furniture that matters. Think again. I promise you that one of these answer cards can make a set with the other three."

(Ask the class to volunteer possible ideas for the right criterion to apply.)

"I see it now!" Max exclaimed. "It has to do with their legs! All the furniture pieces have four legs, and so does the Great Dane! None of the other animals has four legs. The Great Dane must be the best answer!"

Just then Isabel the Inventor scampered into the hollow of the oak tree. "Hi, Jordan and Max. You're playing cards! May I play, too?"

"Sure, Isabel" replied Jordan, and he dealt out the next hand. *(Place **Jordan's Cards 4** on the overhead projector.)*

"Well," began Max cautiously. "Since EACH card has a diamond and a circle on it, we need to think of more criteria. We might want to consider that one shape is dark and the other shape is light in each of the set cards. If we use that for a criterion, then Card 2 doesn't work. In addition, in our set, each circle and diamond are overlapping. Using that for a criterion eliminates Cards 4 and 5!" Max was getting excited. "And look at how the shapes in the set cards are centered in the middle! It's Card 3, right?"

"Using those criteria, then Card 3 certainly works," approved Jordan. "What do you think, Isabel?"

Isabel was still quietly studying the cards. "You know how I always like to look at things a little bit differently? Well, look at how all the diamonds in the set cards are taller than they are wide. But that's not true of the diamond in Card 3. If I use that for one of my criteria instead of the one about light and dark shapes, then MY best choice is Card 2. That works, too, doesn't it, Jordan?"

"Indeed it does, Isabel," replied Jordan. "What's so important to remember here is that the best choice will always depend upon what criteria you choose to use. Changing the criteria will often change your answer!"

"I like this game!" exclaimed Max. "It's definitely different! Let's play a few more hands!"

Jordan's Cards 1

Jordan's Cards 2

Jordan's Cards 3

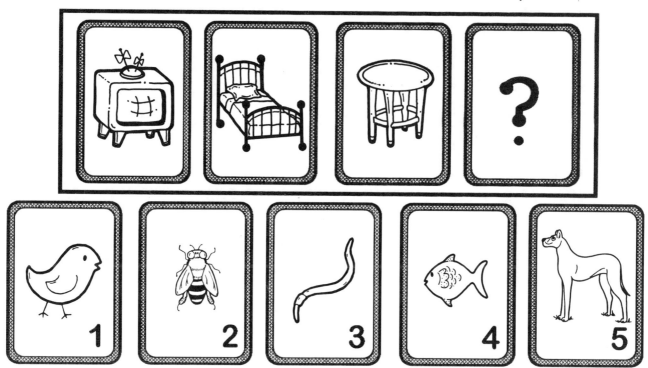

Jordan's Cards 4

Name _____

Quintessential Sets 1

Circle the card that you think best fits in each set.
What criteria (or considerations) did you use?

My criteria:

_____

_____

_____

My criteria:

_____

_____

_____

My criteria:

_____

_____

_____

Quintessential Sets 2

Circle the card that you think best fits in each set.
What criteria (or considerations) did you use?

  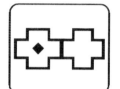 

My criteria:

_____
_____
_____

My criteria:

_____
_____
_____

My criteria:

_____
_____
_____

EVALUATIVE THINKING
SMALL GROUP
LESSON 1

PURPOSE

The purpose of this lesson is to practice creating measurable, factual criterion questions and applying them on a creative problem-solving matrix.

MATERIALS

— a selection of student backpacks borrowed from students not in the group
   Five to eight backpacks make a good assortment.
   Select backpacks with a wide variety of different qualities such as
   fabrics, styles, closures, extra pockets, etc.
— a duplicated class set of *Backpack Bonanza!*
— a copy of *PETS™ Small Group Checklist* for each student

LESSON PLAN

1. Prior to meeting with the group, borrow backpacks from other students. Choose unique backpack styles when possible, gathering a variety of styles, fabrics, and closures. Number the backpacks by placing sticky pad labels or masking tape on them. Try to collect at least five backpacks, but eight or ten is not too many. Place backpacks in the back of the room or another location where they will not be readily evident to the students.

2. Ask students what makes a good backpack. Record all ideas in a list where students can see it. Possible ideas may include the following:

— straps of sturdy material
— wide, padded straps for comfort
— many small pockets for storage
— drawstring closure inside the top flap
— zippers vs. Velcro®
— a loop for hanging the backpack inside a locker
— adjustable straps

3. When the ideas seem exhausted, give students *Backpack Bonanza!* Ask students to select the five ideas from the criteria list that they feel are the most important to them and to write them on their matrix in measurable question form. For example: "Which backpack has the sturdiest closures?" or "Which backpack is the roomiest?" Allow each student to choose whichever criteria he or she feels is the most important.

4. When students have completed their criterion questions, working individually, have each student take his or her matrix to the area with the backpacks. Tell each student that these 10 backpacks are on display at the local variety store. Which five would they be interested in examining more closely? They should place these five numbers on the rows on their matrices.

5. Have each student work individually to compare each backpack according to his or her five chosen criteria. Students may discuss and compare ideas, but each should complete his or her own matrix. Have students circle the highest total on their completed matrices and then discuss as a group which backpack seemed favored by most.

DIAGNOSTIC NOTES

Note students who are fluent or creative while brainstorming criterion ideas, capable of turning criterion ideas into measurable, objective criterion questions, able to apply the criteria in completing their matrices objectively, and/or are able to see others' viewpoints throughout the lesson.

NOTES

Name _____

Backpack Bonanza!

FACTS

FACTS

These backpacks are on display at the local variety store.

You need a new backpack.

Problem-Solving Matrix	**CRITERIA**					**SCORING COLUMN**
Which backpack would be the best one to buy? Write 4 criteria that will help you choose the best backpack. List them in this row. List the numbers of 5 of the backpacks below in this column.	1.	2.	3.	4.		
1.						
2.						
3.						
4.						
5.						

PROBLEM

SOLUTIONS

Matrix©Dodie Merritt

EVALUATIVE THINKING
SMALL GROUP
LESSON 2

PURPOSE

The purpose of this lesson is to evaluate the overall benefit of a decision through its positive and negative outcomes.

MATERIALS

— large butcher paper, one for the demonstration *A Future's Wheel: Bigger Engines* and one sheet for each group of three or four students
— red and green markers for each group of students
— a copy of *PETS™ Small Group Checklist* for each student

LESSON PLAN

1. Prior to the small group lesson, prepare the butcher paper. To prepare the demonstration *A Future's Wheel: Bigger Engines* draw a large circle in the center of the paper and write *Bigger Engines* in it using any color of marker other than red or green.

To prepare the butcher paper for students, draw a large circle in the center of each sheet. Using any colored marker other than red or green, write *School Uniform* in the center of each circle. Set these papers aside until after the demonstration of *A Future's Wheel*. When the students are ready to do their own Future's Wheels, they will need a large work area and, if possible, a red and green marker for each student.

2. To begin the lesson, tell students they are going to apply their evaluative thinking by using a process called Future's Wheels. Explain any important decision probably has positive and negative outcomes. A Future's Wheel is designed to help them see the pros and cons of a decision in order to evaluate the overall benefit of the decision. Use the provided demonstration *A Future's Wheel: Bigger Engines* or create your own.

3. Future's Wheel Demonstration: Begin by explaining the scenario that cars these days have much bigger, more powerful engines than they used to have, as stated in the center hub of the wheel. Point out that this scenario will have both positive and negative ramifications.

Ideas on the positive side of the issue will be recorded on the wheel in green, and ideas on

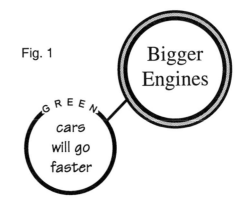

Fig. 1

the negative side will be recorded in red. For example, bigger, more powerful engines allow cars to go faster. This is positive and should be recorded on the wheel in green (fig. 1). Use one spoke to attach this idea to the wheel, since it comes directly from the main hub.

In addition, more powerful engines mean cars use more fuel. This is generally negative and should be recorded in red (fig. 2) Since it comes directly from the main hub idea, it should be attached with one spoke. The main hub can have as many ideas attached to it as the students can brainstorm.

The ideas in the spokes of the wheel may spark controversy, too. The ideas coming from these new hubs will have two spokes to attach them, since they are now twice removed from the original hub. For example, since cars can now go faster, people are able to travel more. Most people would view this as a good thing, so it should be recorded in green (fig. 3).

However, faster cars also mean more serious accidents. This is negative and should be recorded in red with two spokes (fig. 4).

Students may also see that more travel can mean that parents will spend more time away from home traveling on the job. This negative idea would be recorded in red, and since it is now three times removed from the original hub, it would be attached with three spokes (fig. 5).

On the other hand, being able to travel more may mean being able to take more exotic vacations. This positive idea should be attached with three spokes, too, but recorded in green.

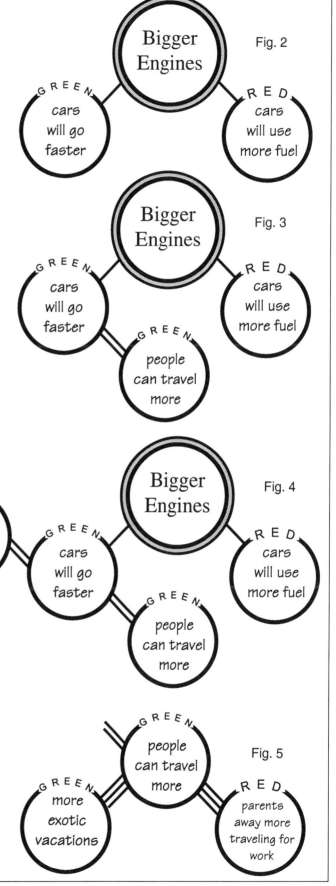

And so on, with students generating as many pertinent consequences as they can and attaching them to the appropriate hub with the appropriate number of spokes for about 10 or 15 minutes. Having demonstrated the process to the students, do not discuss with them the overall impression left by the Future's Wheel until after students have done their own Future's Wheels.

4. Have students work in small groups of three or four to create their own Future's Wheel. Tell them that the principal is considering having all students begin wearing school uniforms next year. (If your school already has school uniforms, then an alternate scenario will be needed.) Ask the students to discuss as a group the pros and cons of this idea and to record their thoughts on their butcher paper charts in a Future's Wheel format.

5. At the end of the group time, hold the charts up and determine whether the papers are mostly red or mostly green. If a paper is mostly red, then the group thought the idea was not a good one overall; if it is mostly green, then the group liked the idea overall. It is important that the students see that although their paper will undoubtedly have both colors on it, they are looking for an OVERALL perception of the idea. Also be sure to de-brief the students at the end of the group time by telling them that this was just an exercise; the school is not planning to switch to uniforms. OR...if the groups thought this would be a good idea, they could put their plan into action by composing a letter to the school principal. Students may take the activity more seriously if they believe it is a possible scenario.

DIAGNOSTIC NOTES

Listen for students who can support their opinions with factual criteria. Listen also for students who are able to see both sides of the issue and can value other viewpoints, even if they do not agree with them. Delaying judgment until the very end is also an important consideration.

NOTES

EVALUATIVE THINKING
SMALL GROUP
LESSON 3

PURPOSE

The purpose of this lesson is to practice evaluative thinking in combination with visual thinking by choosing which shape best fits a particular title.

MATERIALS

— a duplicated class set of *What's the Best Fit for a Bizmot?*
— a duplicated class set of *Bizmots & More*
— a duplicated class set of *Bizmots & More 2*
— scissors and glue for student use
— a copy of *PETS™ Small Group Checklist* for each student

LESSON PLAN

1. Review the characteristics of evaluative thinking:
    — Decisions are based on factual, observable criteria.
    — There is no one right solution.
    — The objective is to determine the best solution from a series of choices.

2. Distribute the materials to each student. From the 8 pictures, students are to select one which in their minds best fits each of the eight names given for the pictures. Students are to cut out the shapes they select, glue them in the appropriately titled boxes, and write three criteria for each of their selections.

3. It is not imperative that students come up with three criteria. Do not allow rules to overshadow the main purpose of the lesson. It is better to have one **factual and observable** criterion than several weak criteria based on nothing or on opinion only. Possible criterion statements include:
    — This design is the best "Wivverly" because wivverly sounds as if it suggests a shimmery, wavy shape and this shape is the waviest.
    — This design is the best "Wivverly" because it reminds me of a giant W, and Wivverly is the only name that begins with a W.

Some of the best criterion statements will be created by the students themselves.

Examples of poor criterion statements include:

— This design is the best "Wivverly" because I like it the best from those in the group.
— This design is the best "Wivverly" because I think it looks like a Wivverly would look.

4. Students do not need to maintain the orientation of a picture as it is presented in the book. Allow them to rotate the pictures as much as they wish in order to come up with their selections.

DIAGNOSTIC NOTES

This lesson is very interesting because it does not always yield impressive results, but when desired results are evident, it will "stop you in your tracks." Look for students who are able to apply factual, observable criteria in their selection process and avoid relying solely on their opinions.

Look also for the student who sees things a bit differently, whose perspective is one not considered before, but upon looking at it from the student's point of view, his or her selection is quite sound and may in fact be extremely original. As more samplings of this activity are collected, good visual and evaluative thinking at work will become easier to recognize.

NOTES

What's the Best Fit for a Bizmot?

Max the Magician is creating a new card trick to entertain his friends in Crystal Pond Woods. However, he cannot decide which name best fits each shape on his new cards.

How would you match up the names and shapes?
What would your criteria (or considerations) be for each match?

Max's New Cards

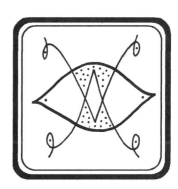

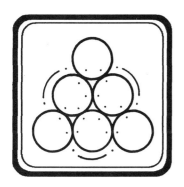

Name _____

Bizmots & More

Which name best fits the shape on each of Max the Magician's new cards?
Why? List 3 criteria (considerations) for each of your choices.

BIZMOT	1.
	2.
	3.
DURFULRINGER	1.
	2.
	3.
HOPSHANDLE	1.
	2.
	3.
PLURB	1.
	2.
	3.

Name _____

Bizmots & More 2

Which name best fits the shape on each of Max the Magician's new cards?
Why? List 3 criteria (considerations) for each of your choices.

	1.
	2.
NAZROD	3.
	1.
	2.
SNERT	3.
	1.
	2.
ZABLONK	3.
	1.
	2.
ZINGZANGER	3.

DUDLEY THE DETECTIVE

© Dodie Merritt

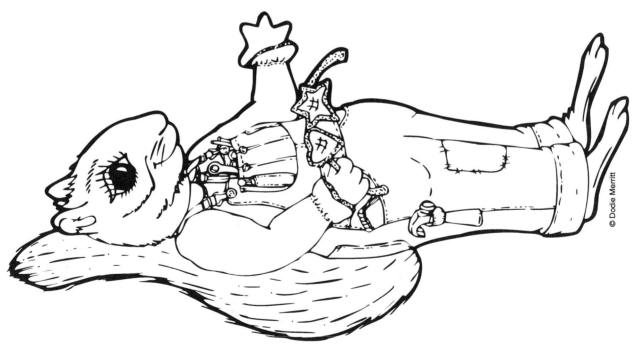

ISABEL THE INVENTOR

© Dodie Merritt

190

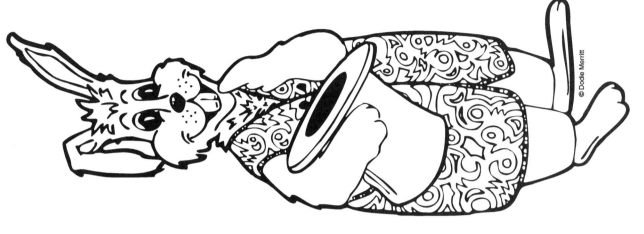

MAX THE MAGICIAN

© Dodie Merritt

SYBIL THE SCIENTIST

© Dodie Merritt

JORDAN THE JUDGE

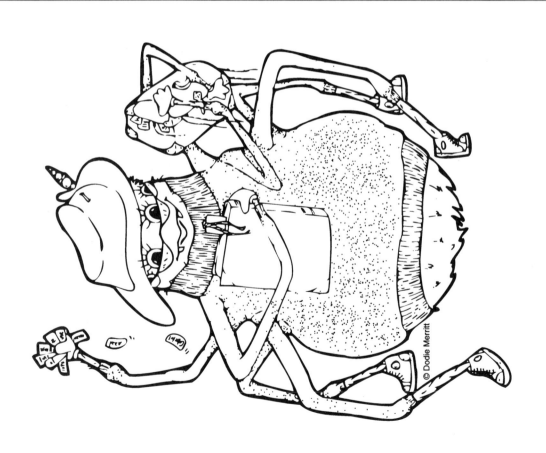

YOLANDA THE YARNSPINNER

192